Drinking Water

NUMBER TWENTY-ONE:

Louise Lindsey Merrick Natural Environment Series

Drinking Water

Refreshing Answers
to All Your Questions

by James M. Symons

Illustrations by

Maria Leticia Ramirez

TEXAS A&M UNIVERSITY PRESS

College Station

This expanded and updated book is based on *Plain Talk about Drinking Water: Answers to 101 Important Questions about the Water You Drink*, first published by the American Water Works Association in 1992.

The paper used in this book meets the minimum requirements of the American National Standard for Permanence of Paper for Printed Library Materials, Z39.48-1984. Binding materials have been chosen for durability.

Library of Congress Cataloging-in-Publication Data

Symons, James M.
    Drinking water : refreshing answers to all your questions / James M. Symons.
        p. cm. — (Louise Lindsey Merrick natural environment series ; no. 21)
    Includes index.
    ISBN 0-89096-646-X. — ISBN 0-89096-659-1 (pbk.)
    1. Drinking water—Miscellanea. 2. Water quality—Miscellanea. I. Title. II. Series.
TD353.S957 1995
363.6'1—dc20   94-39842
                                                                        CIP

To my wife, Joan, and to our children, Andy, Linda, and Julie, for their patience throughout the years; and to my mother and father for their lifelong support

Contents

Preface

During my professional career, I have received many telephone calls from people concerned about their drinking water. In addition, friends, neighbors, and relatives have sought answers from me about the water they drink. This curiosity is understandable and proper, as drinking water is so vital to life, yet to many people it is a mystery—where does it come from; is it safe; what about newspaper and magazine articles that describe the hazards of drinking water; are advertised products for the home any good?

I prepared answers to the most common of these questions and presented them in a book called *Plain Talk about Drinking Water*, which was published by the American Water Works Association. The American Water Works Association and its 55,000 members work to assure a safe, sufficient supply of drinking water for the people of North America. The group leads efforts to advance the science and technology of drinking water, as well as the management of water utilities. It also promotes consumer awareness and influences government policies related to drinking water. Its members are united with one common goal—to provide drinking water of unquestionable quality.

Plain Talk sold more than 38,000 copies, and in 1994, with media coverage of drinking water problems on the upswing, I set about expanding, updating, and reorganizing the book for a wider audience in the United States and Canada. The resulting book, titled *Drinking Water: Refreshing Answers to All Your Questions*, presents the facts in nontechnical language for the average reader, making it easy to become an informed consumer. As an additional aid to the reader, the few scientific terms used are followed by a phonetic guide at their first appearance. The questions are organized by categories; for example, all questions relating to the health (safety) aspects of drinking water are in one section of the book. The index makes finding the answers to your specific concerns still easier. In addition, a list of references and two appendices— one listing sources of additional information, the other listing the questions themselves—are included. The list of questions provides an easy way to quickly get an overview of all the questions in a section or to locate a particular question. Some questions and answers are related; in these instances, cross-references are provided at the end of the answers to help you locate the related topics.

One note of caution: although I have made every attempt to be accurate, these answers must be general in nature; thus, I cannot cover all variances caused by local conditions. Wherever possible, I suggest additional sources of information for these.

In addition, although most of the material is generic, some information is specific to conditions in the United States, Canada, or both. I appreciate the assistance provided by Ken Roberts of the Ontario Ministry of the Environment and his staff, who provided information on the Canadian situation in the answers to several of the questions.

No project like this can be completed alone. I would like to thank my friends and relatives who helped ensure that my answers were understandable to the general public: Marianne and Bill Myers, Lisa and Andy Symons, Linda Raab, Joan Symons, Nancy Logsdon, and Doug McIlroy.

I am also grateful to the professional colleagues who assisted me: Ray Taylor, Gary Logsdon, Tom Sorg, Mike Schock, Ed Geldreich, Irwin Kugelman, Jim Kreissl, Louis Simms, Warren Norris, Bob Hoehn, Jack Matson, Tom Pankratz, Roger Eichhorn, Dennis Clifford, Wendell LaFoe, Raanana Levin, Susan Gregory, Joe Harrison, Mark Dickson, Tom Love, Vanessa Libby, Dick van der Koiij (who provided me the book *Laus Aquae*, from which the quotes that open each chapter were taken), Ed Ohanian, M. G. Christie, Mead Noss, Ric

Jensen, Bill Lauer, George Symons, John Hoff, Roger Hulbert, Monica Baruth, Ron Packham, Katie McCain, Bill Knocke, and Ted Cleveland. In addition, I am indebted to the California Water Service Company for giving me permission to use some material from *Straight Talk on Water Quality*, a question-and-answer booklet for its customers.

I wish to thank my reviewers of the second edition of *Plain Talk about Drinking Water*—Jack W. Hoffbuhr, C. William Myers, Thomas J. Sorg, and Raymond H. Taylor—and the publisher's reviewer of this manuscript, each of whom contributed much of their valuable time to assist me and to improve the final product. My proofreaders, Charlene Baker and Joan Symons, generously gave of their time in assisting me; I thank them.

Finally, I acknowledge many at the American Water Works Association who helped me with the original publication, particularly Nancy Zeilig, Mary Kay Kozyra, and Norm Udevitz. This project was fun for me; I hope it is informative and entertaining reading for you.

How the Water Spirit Got Her Power

Once, long ago, Sun was the ruler of all the earth. Next to him, the other spirits were as the sparrow beside the grizzly bear. So the spirits had a secret meeting and elected the water-spirit to approach the Sun to give up some of his power.

Water went to Sun, and formed a clear, deep pool at his feet. When Sun saw his own face reflected in the pool, he was so delighted that he promised Water anything she wanted. When she demanded some of his power, he realized that he had been tricked, but according to his word, he gave power to all of the other spirits. Water, for her part, got more than anyone, and became, next to Sun, the most powerful force on earth.

—From a plaque next to Takakkaw Falls,
Yoho National Park, British Columbia, Canada

Drinking Water

1.

Health

Of this we may be sure: man must eat to live, and the problem of food will always be inextricably associated with water.

—Thompson King, *Water, Miracle of Nature*

GENERAL

1. *"Is my water safe to drink?"*

A definitive answer for countries as large as the United States and Canada is impossible, of course, but for the most part, yes. Nearly all the water supplies in the United States meet the U.S. Environmental Protection Agency's standards for safe drinking water.

However, small water systems have more trouble meeting these standards than do larger cities. For example, in 1990 in the United States, 9.5 percent of the 51,654 smaller water suppliers (serving populations of 3,300 or less) violated standards for germs in their drinking water. NOTE: *The term* **germ** *is used to describe disease-producing microbes (very tiny organisms that can be seen only with a microscope). The scientific term for germ is* **pathogen** *(PATH·o·gin).* Less than one percent of the larger systems had similar violations. Records are not kept on the quality of private wells used by individual households. Smaller utilities frequently have a small tax base, so they often have difficulty raising money if corrections are needed. Problems can therefore arise.

Similar problems exist in Canada, especially in the smaller municipal supplies, where poorer-quality source water is often used. Specific statistics are not available.

Periodically, reports appear in the media indicating that tap water is not safe to drink in many locations because the local utilities have violated one or more of the rules of the U.S. Environmental Protection Agency. "Rules are rules" and they all should be obeyed, but they do not all have the same implications for the *quality* of drinking water.

For example, if a water supplier does not test the water as frequently as called for in the rules, this is a violation. This type of violation does not necessarily mean that the water quality is poor; it *does*, however, mean that the utility does not know enough about the quality of the water. Also, having too much of a chemical in the water for a short time before corrections can be made is not an immediate cause for alarm, as all the limits for chemicals in the water are set with large safety factors included. Germs, of course, are another matter and should be eliminated immediately. Media reports of violations must be studied carefully. If you're concerned, your local water supplier can tell you about its compliance record, and if there are problems, what they are going to do about them.

(See Questions 11, 13, 95, 112, and 115 for related information.)

2. *"Can I tell if my drinking water is okay by just looking at it, tasting it, or smelling it?"* No. None of the chemicals or microbes that could make you sick can be seen, tasted, or smelled.

(See Question 39 for related information.)

3. *"How do I find out if my water is safe to drink?"* If you do not have your own private well, you can telephone your water supplier and ask if the water meets the federal, state, or provincial standards. You can also ask your city, county, state, or provincial health department. In the United States, federal law states that consumers must be notified if violations of regulations occur. Canadian law does not require violations to be reported to consumers. If you have your own private well, you are responsible for having it tested yourself. Once it has been tested, you can discuss the results with your local health department.

4. *"I've received a notice from my water utility telling me that something is wrong. What's that all about? What is a 'boil water order?'"* In the United States, if a supplier violates any federal drinking water standard, the utility, by law, must notify the customer. The idea behind this requirement is that the consumer has a right to know if the supplier is complying with all the standards. All violations are important, of course, but they are not all equally important. For instance, if the problem reported to customers is that the water supplier has not sampled the water as frequently as required by the regulations, this does not *necessarily* mean that the quality of the water has dropped.

One violation involving insufficient sampling, improper reporting, or water quality does not mean the water is unsafe to drink. It does mean, however, that the water utility should improve its operations. On the other hand, if coliforms (which indicate the possible presence of germs) are found in the drinking water, customers will be issued a **boil water order**—that is, they will be told to boil their water—until further notice. Remember, if you have a boil water order in your area, be sure to throw all of your ice cubes away. They may have been made with contaminated water.

Consumers in Canada would not necessarily be notified of problems, although sometimes provincial health or environmental agencies issue orders for all consumers to boil their drinking water.

(See Questions 11 and 14 for related information.)

5. *"Does anyone actually get sick from drinking water?"*

Each year from 1970 to 1990, about 7,700 cases of sickness in the United States were traced directly to drinking water. These illnesses (usually characterized by vomiting and diarrhea) were most often caused by improper treatment of the water. Deaths were rare. Between 1980 and 1990, 62 percent of the waterborne-disease outbreaks occurred in water systems that were improperly disinfected (a process to kill germs) or not disinfected at all. In Canada, between 1974 and 1984, 51 waterborne-disease outbreaks involving 3,799 people were reported. In contrast, a recent Environment Ministry's study in Russia reported that one-third of their 148 million people get sick every year from the drinking water.

A waterborne-disease outbreak that occurred in Milwaukee, Wisconsin, in the spring of 1993 made national news because of the number of people who got sick—several hundred thousand—with some deaths. The germ that caused the problem is called *Cryptosporidium* (krip·toe·spor·ID·eum), an **intestinal protozoa**. From 1986 through 1990, twenty waterborne-disease outbreaks due to intestinal protozoa were reported in the United States. These outbreaks occurred in ten states and affected more than 15,000 people. In response to these incidents, water suppliers using surface water, where these protozoa can occur, are improving treatment.

To be specific, although the U.S. Environmental Protection Agency has not yet changed its standards on surface water treatment—it may in the future—it is recommending that water suppliers treating surface water notify the proper local authorities if the cloudiness of the treated water is above the standard for more than twelve hours. Cloudiness of water is measured by a test for **turbidity** (tur·BID·it·ee), and the water supplier has very sensitive instruments that can detect slight changes in cloudiness, changes you could not detect by looking at the water. Measuring this cloudiness is important, because if it goes up a little, this indicates that treatment effectiveness is declining slightly, and it is at these times that *Cryptosporidium* might slip through the plant and into the drinking water.

The American Water Works Association (AWWA), an organization to which water suppliers belong, is also urging better surface water treatment practices. The current standard for turbidity is 0.5 units. AWWA is recommending that drinking water treatment plants treating surface water should produce water containing only 0.1 unit or less, and that water suppliers should focus on maintaining 100 percent treatment reliability by having backup equipment, chemical feeders, and so forth. All these steps will minimize the possibility of another outbreak such as occurred in Milwaukee.

(See Questions 78 and 93 for related information.)

6. *"I have read about animals dying after drinking reservoir water. If this can happen, how can I be sure my drinking water is safe?"*

Sheep, dogs, birds, or even cattle may die after consuming water heavily laden with a green scum caused by algae (a microscopic plant). Heavy growths (called **blooms**) of algae sometimes occur in reservoirs during warmer weather. Certain types of algae contain toxic chemicals. If the number of algae is high enough, the animals that drink this water can die.

Water suppliers treat their reservoirs to prevent heavy growths of algae and any algae that do get into the water are removed at the water treatment plant. Because algae also cause taste and odor problems, whenever algae are growing in large numbers, the water will be treated (beyond what is described in Question 93) to improve it. This extra treatment will also remove any algal products that might be of concern. To be extra safe, however, water utilities are now studying algal products to make sure they understand and can prevent any problems.

7. *"They let people swim and go boating in our reservoir. Should I worry about this?"*

Although the swimmers and boats do add some pollution, when this pollution is diluted by all the water that is in the lake or reservoir, it doesn't amount to much. In addition, because the water is thoroughly treated before it comes to you, any contamination will have been removed. Fires and litter cause far more trouble than this kind of pollution.

8. *"Is tap water suitable for use in a home kidney dialysis machine?"*

No, not without further treatment. In a kidney dialysis machine, the water used is brought into close contact with the patient's blood. Thus, the quality requirements are far stricter than those for ordinary drinking water. Aluminum, fluoride, and chloramine (CHLOR·uh·mean) are examples of substances that are okay if found in drinking water but are not acceptable in water used for kidney dialysis. Water suppliers cannot be expected to meet these strict requirements, so the water is further treated immediately prior to use in the dialysis machine. Kidney dialysis centers are kept informed about water quality by water suppliers and are able to give advice on this matter.

(See Questions 12, 27, and 30 for related information.)

9. *"Is it true that people who take antacids regularly are more likely to get sick from drinking water?"*

This has not been proven. Because the acid in the stomach that aids digestion tends to kill any germs a person might drink, some health professionals think that antacids, by destroying stomach acid, decrease this natural protection against germ disease. But at the moment, this is just speculation, not fact.

10. *"When I'm working in the yard, I'm tempted to take a drink from my garden hose. Is this safe?"*

No. A standard vinyl garden hose has substances in it to keep the hose flexible. These chemicals, which get into the water as it goes through the hose, are not good for you. They are not good for animals or pets, either, so filling drinking containers for them out of a garden hose is not a good idea.

However, one type of hose on the market is made with a "food-grade" plastic that is approved by the U.S. Food and Drug Administration and will not contaminate the water. Campers with recreational vehicles should use this type of hose when hooking up to a drinking water tap at a campsite.

GERMS

11. *"Is my drinking water completely free of microbes?"*

No, but don't be alarmed; most microbes are harmless. For example, if you licked your finger, you would get microbes in your mouth, but you wouldn't get sick. Drinking water contains these harmless microbes. It should be, and probably is, free of germs, however. Because most water is germ-free, many pediatricians in metropolitan areas do not think it is necessary to boil tap water used in making baby formula.

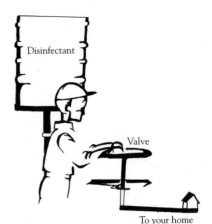

12. *"How are germs that can make me sick kept out of my drinking water?"*

A chemical called a **disinfectant** is added to drinking water at the treatment plant. Chlorine is the most common disinfectant used in the United States and Canada. In the United States, chlorine is used in 75 percent of the larger systems and 95 percent of the smaller ones. Almost all the rest use a close relative of chlorine called chloramine. Chlorine and chloramine kill germs but do not harm humans. Your water supplier can tell you what is used in your water.

Although most private well waters are germ-free, and thus they usually are not disinfected, they should always be tested at least once—annually is better—to uncover any possible germ contamination.

Some germs—for example, *Cryptosporidium*—are very difficult to kill with a disinfectant. This type of germ is not found in groundwater, and most water suppliers who use surface water, where this type of germ can be found, depend on filtration for removing them.

(See Questions 29, 78, 93, and 117 for related information.)

13. *"I'm told that I shouldn't drink my well water or that I need to boil it because my water has coliforms in it, but I'm also told that coliforms are harmless. Then I read that food poisoning can occur because of coliforms in meat. What are coliforms, and what's going on?"*

Coliforms generally are harmless bacteria (a type of microbe) that live naturally in the intestines of humans, aiding in the functioning of the body.

Water that contains coliforms is *not* safe to drink, however not because of the coliforms, but because of the germs that possibly may be in well water when coliforms are found there. (Germs live in the body in the same place as the coliforms.) In fact, coliform organisms are called **indicator organisms** because their presence indicates the possibility of germ contamination.

NOTE: *A few types of coliform bacteria do act as germs and cannot be ignored. These bacterial germs, called intestinal pathogenic* **Escherichia** *(esh·uh·*RIK·*i·uh)* **coli** *by scientists (E. coli for short), have caused several food-borne and waterborne outbreaks of disease, with the loss of life primarily among senior citizens and young children. Fortunately, such occurrences are rare.*

(See Question 4 for related information.)

14. *"If I want to kill all the germs in my drinking water, what should I do?"*

Using a timer, bring the water to a full boil on a stove or in a microwave oven, then boil it for one minute. Because the boiling temperature of water goes down about two degrees for each 1,000 feet you live above sea level, people living at high altitudes should increase the boiling time. For example, in Denver, which is over 5,000 feet above sea level, boiling time should be increased to three minutes.

Treating water in this way should be done only in emergencies, because heating and boiling use a lot of energy and concentrate some chemicals (nitrates and pesticides) if they are in the drinking water. However, the advantage of killing the germs outweighs the slight disadvantage of concentrating the chemicals, which results in only a minor worsening of water quality.

15. *"Could my drinking water transmit the AIDS virus?"*

There is absolutely no evidence that AIDS can be transmitted through drinking water. There is no danger from drinking water for three reasons. First, and most important, you can't get AIDS by drinking the virus, it must get into the blood directly. Second, the virus is very weak outside the body and rapidly becomes noninfectious. Finally, even if present in water sources, the virus is easily killed during the disinfection step of drinking water treatment.

CHEMICALS

General

16. *"Are all chemicals in my drinking water bad for me?"*

No. Some chemicals, for example fluoride, are good for you, and some minerals are accepted by most to be beneficial in drinking water. In addition, many chemicals have no bad effect on your health.

Chemicals are not bad just because they are chemicals. For example, water itself is a chemical, and we depend on chemicals in food to keep us alive.

(See Question 27 for related information.)

17. *"Are chemicals that are found in drinking water naturally (rather than because of pollution) nontoxic?"*

Not necessarily. Many chemicals that occur in nature can be harmful to your health, and they can be present in water. A few examples are arsenic, radium, radon, and selenium. Also, some nontoxic natural chemicals combine with other chemicals to produce harmful chemicals (**reaction products**). Therefore, some "natural" chemicals must be watched closely by your water supplier. The U.S. Environmental Protection Agency has developed a list of nearly ninety chemicals the water supplier must test for. Some of these are "natural"; others are caused by human activity.

(See Questions 29 and 39 for related information.)

18. *"I read that organic chemicals are bad for my health. What are they, why are they dangerous, and why doesn't my water utility just remove them?"*

Organic chemicals have mostly carbon atoms connected to hydrogen atoms (the element, not the gas). A common organic chemical in the home is sugar, so not all organic chemicals are dangerous. Food contains many beneficial organic chemicals essential to our life. NOTE: *You can't tell if something is an organic chemical just by looking at it.* For example, table salt looks a lot like sugar but does not contain carbon and hydrogen, so is an **inorganic** chemical.

Dangerous organic chemicals are found in products like gasoline, cleaning fluid, pesticides, paint thinners, and car radiator fluid. They are dangerous if they get into your drinking water because many are cancer-causing chemicals — called **carcinogens** (car·SIN·o·jins). The water treatment methods used by most utilities are designed to make drinking water clear and to kill germs. These treatment systems can't remove organic chemicals, which require different treatment methods. To improve protection from these and other chemicals, the future may bring changes in the way suppliers treat drinking water. (In fact, the U.S. Environmental Protection Agency regulates many of these chemicals, and where new treatment methods are needed, some water suppliers are using them already, and this trend will continue.)

(See Questions 12 and 93 for related information.)

19. "I'm told that our drinking water contains chemicals like cleaning fluid and benzene. What can I do about this while the water company is improving treatment?"

These chemicals are called **solvents**. The best thing to do is boil your water for ten minutes (use a timer), either on the stove or in a microwave oven. About 20 percent of the volume will be lost during boiling, and this may concentrate other pollutants like nitrates and pesticides. Boil the water in a well-ventilated area. Mixing with an electric, eggbeater-type mixer for ten minutes is also very effective, since vigorous mixing causes some of the chemicals to evaporate. Storing water in an open pan for forty-eight hours will also work. Aeration with an aquarium-type aerator or pouring the water back and forth between two containers are other treatments, but less effective. Using an aerated faucet is ineffective. A more expensive option is to use bottled water as a temporary remedy (see Questions 59 and 60).

These methods need to be considered only if the water company notifies you that the levels of solvents in your water exceed the drinking water standards.

20. *"I've heard that nitrates are bad for infants and pesticides are bad for everyone. How do nitrates and pesticides get into my drinking water?"*

The U.S. Environmental Protection Agency sets a limit for nitrates because high levels are associated with a rare blood condition in infants—commonly called the blue-baby syndrome because the baby's skin turns bluish after the baby drinks water containing nitrates. Nitrate concentration has been a problem in some private wells. Nitrates and pesticides come from fertilizers and pesticides used on farms and on home gardens and lawns. Septic tank drain fields and wastes from animal feedlots are other important sources of nitrates. As rainwater passes down through the ground, it takes these chemicals with it and contaminates the groundwater. During this movement, microbes in the soil change the ammonia in the fertilizer and drainage from septic tanks and feedlots into nitrates.

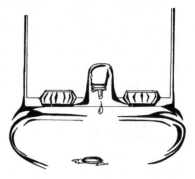

21. *"There is a blue-green stain where my water drips into my sink. What causes this?"*

This stain comes from the chemical copper. The copper probably is present in your home plumbing and is being dissolved into the drinking water. The conditions that cause copper in the water also can introduce lead into drinking water, and high amounts of either lead or copper can cause health problems. If you have blue-green stains in your sink, you should call your local water supplier to discuss this. If your water is from a private well, have your tap water tested for lead and copper.

To clean the sink, check with your local hardware store for stain removal products.

(See Question 23 for related information.)

22. *"Do hazardous wastes contaminate drinking water?"*

Yes, they may. As rainwater seeps down through a hazardous waste dump, it carries the chemicals with it to the groundwater. Some chemicals stick to the dirt particles and don't reach the groundwater very quickly. Other chemicals, like cleaning fluid or gasoline, move down through the ground rapidly. Leaking under-

ground gasoline tanks at gas stations and the improper disposal of chemicals (for example, dumping old radiator fluid, metal degreasers, paint thinners, or paintbrush cleaners in the backyard) also may contaminate groundwater. Rain can also wash contaminants from a hazardous waste dump into surface waters, which can then seep into the groundwater and pollute it.

Surface waters in some regions are also contaminated by chemicals used for deicing roads in the winter. When it rains or the snow and ice melt, these chemicals wash into rivers, lakes, and reservoirs. Improperly treated wastes from industrial plants may also pollute surface waters.

(See Questions 57, 85, and 89 for related information.)

Lead

23. *"How does lead get into my drinking water?"*

Not all drinking water contains lead. Where lead is present in pipes and in soldered connections, the lead may dissolve into the water while the water is not moving, generally overnight or at other times when the water supply is not used for several hours. Faucets with brass or bronze internal parts may also be a major source of lead under these conditions. The first water that comes from the faucet after long periods of nonuse may have lead in it. Hard water (see Question 54) sometimes picks up less lead than soft water because hard water has a tendency to lay down a scale layer on the inside of pipes. In the United States, lead is now banned in pipes and in solder, and the voluntary standard for lead in faucets will cause the plumbing industry to change manufacturing methods. However, the piping systems in many cities and faucets still contain lead. Also, the ban on lead-based solder is inconsistently enforced. Consumers should insist that no plumbing repairs be done with lead-based solder and that it not be used in new homes.

In 1991, the U.S. Environmental Protection Agency issued a new regulation for controlling lead in drinking water. If high amounts are found at the tap, corrective action by the supplier is required and public education materials accepted by the EPA must be delivered to customers. In addition, the water supplier must offer to sample the tap water of any customer who requests it. The water supplier, however, is not required to pay for collecting or analyzing the sample, nor is the system required to collect and analyze the sample itself.

Canada banned the use of lead pipe and lead-based solder in 1990 and currently has a proposed guideline of 0.01 milligrams of lead per liter (abbreviated mg/L —see Question 113 for definition) of water in a sample collected from a flowing tap.

(See Questions 54 and 55 for related information.)

24. *"How can I get lead out of my drinking water?"*

Not all homes have a lead problem, but if testing has indicated a problem, if you think your water is corrosive, or if you have rusty water or blue-green stains in your sink, take the following precautions.

Whenever water has not been used for a long period of time — overnight or during the day if no one is home — let the cold water run from the faucet for two minutes (this is a long time) before using any water for drinking or cooking (see Note below). Saving this water for other purposes such as plant watering is a good conservation measure. Letting the water run for two minutes will not flush out all the lead that got into the water while it was sitting in your plumbing, but it will improve the situation greatly.

Some home treatment equipment (sometimes called lead removing filters) does remove lead dissolved in water but, unfortunately, manufacturers' claims are not always accurate, so be cautious and check with independent organizations.

You can get information on lead hazards by calling the National Lead Information Center (see Appendix A).

NOTE: *It is difficult to know how long it takes the "fresh" water from the street pipes to arrive at the faucet. The time needed varies depending on your specific location, water pressure, whether you live in a single-family home or an apartment, and so forth.*

If the water from your cold water faucet gets colder after its run for a while, always leave it open until you feel the colder water. Otherwise, two minutes is usually enough for most homes. Flushing a toilet doesn't work; you must run the faucet you are actually going to use for drinking or cooking.

(See Questions 42 and 51 for related information.)

25. *"How can I find out if my water is supplied through lead pipes?"*

The water main in the road will not be made of lead — usually it's cement-lined cast iron or sometimes plastic — but the pipe connecting it to your house or the pipes within your house might be. Lead pipes are unlikely to be found in newer housing, as their use has been banned since 1986. Plastic is quite common now.

In older homes, however, the pipes might be lead, cop-per, or galvanized iron. Joints on lead pipes are usually very bulky compared with the relatively neat fittings of copper and galvanized iron. You can tell copper by the color (like a penny), but you might have to scrape off some paint to see the actual pipe material. Copper and galvanized iron give a more metallic sound when gently tapped with a small hammer. If you are in doubt, you should consult a reputable plumber.

26. *"Is it safe to drink water from a drinking fountain?"*

Yes, usually. Some older, floor-standing water coolers contain lead-lined storage tanks, and there is a possibil-ity that high amounts of lead could get into the water in these tanks. The U.S. Congress passed laws banning the use of lead in piping and in solder (in 1986) and in storage tanks (in 1988), and these regulations have im-proved the situation. One section of the 1988 act en-courages schools and day-care centers to test their fountains for lead. Canada banned the use of lead in pipes and of lead solder in 1990.

Letting the water run for a while before drinking from a drinking fountain minimizes the risk. How-ever, because the storage tanks are about one quart in size, complete flushing may take a while.

Fluoride

27. *"Is the fluoride in my drinking water safe?"*

Yes. When added or naturally present in the correct amounts, fluoride in drinking water has greatly improved the dental health of American and Canadian consumers. Early studies suggesting that fluoride was a possible cancer-causing chemical proved to be incorrect. A 1993 report by the National Research Council of the National Academy of Sciences, *Health Risk of Ingested Fluoride*, states, "Currently allowed fluoride levels in drinking water do not pose a risk of health problems such as cancer, kidney failure, or bone disease." *Excess* fluoride in water is removed by the water supplier using special treatment.

When present even in correct amounts, fluoride and the disinfectant chloramine do make water unsuitable for use in kidney dialysis machines. Dialysis patients should check with their water supplier or dialysis center about their source of water.

(See Questions 8 and 16 for related information.)

Chlorine

28. *"Is water with chlorine in it safe to drink?"*

Yes. Many tests have shown that the amount of chlorine found in treated water is safe to drink, although some people object to the taste.

(See Questions 39, 40, 51, and 59 for related information.)

29. *"What is the link between chlorine and cancer?"*

Chlorine is added to drinking water to kill germs. While chlorine does provide this protection, though, it also can combine with naturally occurring nontoxic chemicals to form compounds that may cause cancer. The results are called **reaction products**.

Specifically, the U.S. Environmental Protection Agency calls them **disinfection by-products**, or DBPs for short, because they are formed by the germ-killing chemicals (disinfectants). Expect to see stricter limits on DBPs during the last half of the 1990s. Although drinking water treatment is changing to avoid the problem of reaction products, disinfection must remain adequate to kill the germs found in water. Any harmful effects to humans from DBPs are very small and difficult to measure in comparison with the risks associated with inadequate disinfection.

At present (1994), the only DBPs regulated by the USEPA are a group of four chemicals with the general name **trihalomethanes** (try·HAL·o·meth·anes), THMs for short. If you have a problem with these reaction products in your water, you will be notified by your supplier. If you're concerned, you can call them and ask whether the total THM level in your water is okay.

(See Questions 5, 12, 17, and 114 for related information.)

Aluminum

30. *"I hear aluminum is used to treat drinking water. Is this a problem? Does it cause Alzheimer's disease?"*

Aluminum-containing chemicals—called alum (AL·um) or aluminum sulfate (SUL·fate)—are used to treat most surface waters (see Question 93). These chemicals trap dirt and then form large particles in the water that settle out; thus, very little aluminum stays in the water.

Considerable publicity was given to some studies suggesting that more people got Alzheimer's disease in areas where drinking water contained small amounts of aluminum. According to most Alzheimer's disease experts, these reports are not accurate. Aluminum is a natural chemical that occurs in many foods, including tea; even if you live in areas where the level of aluminum in drinking water is much above average, your intake from food would be about twenty times your intake from drinking water. Aluminum is not regulated in drinking water in the United States or Canada because there is no reliable evidence that it is dangerous. The province of Ontario, Canada, does have a guideline of 0.100 milligrams per liter (mg/ L—see Question 113 for definition), to prevent white materials from forming in the pipes.

(See Question 8 for related information.)

31. *"Is it safe to cook with aluminum pans?"* Yes. No health problems resulting from cooking with aluminum pans have been proven.

(See Question 8 for related information.)

Radon

32. *"What is radon, and is it harmful in drinking water?"* Radon is a radioactive gas that is dissolved in some groundwaters. It is formed when radium or uranium decays naturally. When inhaled over long periods of time, radon can cause cancer. Currently, experts also think radon has some harmful effects when consumed. When drinking water containing radon is used in your home, some of the radon goes into the air you breathe and the rest remains in the water. The U.S. Environmental Protection Agency will set standards for radon in the mid-1990s, and treatment methods are already available for use by water suppliers if radon removal is required. More radon in air comes from the ground than from drinking water. Testing the air will not determine whether any radon present is seeping out of the ground or is coming from the drinking water.

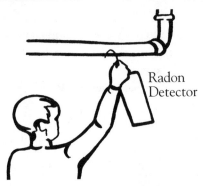

Radon
Detector

33. *"I'm worried that my drinking water has radon in it and that the radon will get into the air in my home. How can I test the air in my home for radon?"*

First, telephone your local health department to find out if it knows whether your drinking water contains radon or if radon is a problem in your area. This will help you decide whether you want to test for radon. The U.S. Environmental Protection Agency recommends that all living areas below the third floor be tested, regardless of location, because its sampling has uncovered high radon levels even in "low-risk" areas.

If you decide that your home should be tested, you can purchase a testing device. Two types of devices are available from hardware and similar stores for prices ranging from thirty to fifty dollars. Both contain prepaid mailing envelopes for sending the detector to a laboratory for testing. The test results then are sent back to you.

One device uses an activated carbon detector. The detector is exposed for several days and then sent to a laboratory. The activated carbon traps radon particles so that they can be counted. The advantage of this device is that you obtain an answer quickly.

The other device uses a film. The radon particles make weak spots in the film. At the laboratory the film is etched to form holes that are counted. This device can be exposed for periods of up to one year. Because radon levels change with time, this long-term testing is an advantage.

Radon gas seeping into a home from underground is a major source of radon in indoor air. Consequently, either type of testing device should be placed in the basement or on the first floor (if your home has no basement) where radon concentrations are likely to be highest.

Two good references are available from the U.S. Environmental Protection Agency: *A Citizen's Guide to Radon* (ANR-464) and *A Home Buyer's and Seller's Guide to Radon* (402-R-93-003). Single copies of both may be obtained free of charge by calling (202) 233-9370.

34. *"Will a water softener take radon and radium out of my water?"*

Radon, no. Radium, yes.

Water softeners are very effective in removing radium, but they do not remove radon. In fact, the radium that is trapped in the water softener will create some radon. Discuss this issue with your water supplier.

Remember that radium is a radioactive element that occurs naturally in some soils and thus in some groundwaters, along with radon.

(See Question 55 for related information.)

TRAVEL

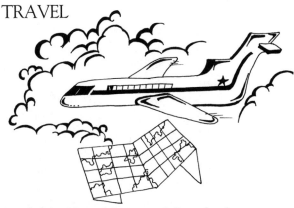

35. *"I travel overseas. In which countries is the water safe to drink?"*

Besides the United States and Canada, the water generally is safe to drink in western Europe, Australia,

New Zealand, and Japan. In other countries, you should insist on carbonated bottled water for drinking and brushing your teeth. Some hotels fill containers with tap water, so be sure you get *carbonated* water. Also, watch out for ice cubes and foods like gelatin that usually are made with tap water. Also beware of salads; the greens are often washed in local tap water.

(See Question 1 for related information.)

36. *"When I travel to a different place in this country, sometimes I have an upset stomach for a couple of days. Is this because something is wrong with the water?"*

This probably does not result from a problem with germs in the drinking water. However, waters with a high mineral content, particularly sulfate, do have a temporary laxative effect, if your body is not accustomed to them. Therefore, the change in mineral content from place to place sometimes does bother travelers for a short time, until the body readjusts.

(See Question 127 for related information.)

37. *"Is it okay for campers, hikers, and backpackers to drink water from remote streams?"*

Although chemical pollution is not a concern in remote streams because a person generally would not drink enough water to cause sickness, the answer is no.

These streams often contain *Giardia*, (jee·AR·dee·uh), a protozoan not a bacteria, and other protozoa such as *Cryptosporidium*, which can cause disease. These two germs cause illnesses called **giardiasis** or **cryptosporidiosis** that is characterized by severe diarrhea, which can last several weeks, sometimes even longer.

In addition, disease-causing bacteria from wildlife might also be present in remote streams.

38. *"What can campers, hikers, and backpackers do to treat stream water to make it safe to drink?"*

Any water that looks good enough to drink can be made microbiologically safe by boiling. One minute of *vigorous* boiling at sea level or three minutes at high elevations will kill all germs, disease-producing bacteria, viruses, protozoan cysts, and so forth.

Water disinfection tablets, available at drugstores and camping supply outlets, can be put into a glass of clear water. They take about five minutes to dissolve and release the disinfectant (see Question 12). These tablets *will not* protect against *Giardia* and *Cryptosporidium* (the primary concerns in most areas) or parasitic worms, however, and will not work well in cloudy or colored water. Thus, their use alone is discouraged.

Some portable water filters available on the market can provide effective treatment. One unit, which resembles a large-diameter soda straw, contains a disinfectant and a filter, as well as other materials. Mouth suction is used to draw clear water through the unit. This filter has not been shown to be very effective, and the small-diameter copies of it work very poorly indeed. Because filters that are designed to remove *Giardia* do not remove the much smaller disease-causing protozoa cysts, bacteria, or viruses (germs), disinfection tablets should be added to the filtered water before use for drinking. The only real answer is to bring your own water or boil the "natural" water.

To avoid other health problems and possible

environmental damage, campers should also be careful about the soaps they use for cleaning. Some can cause dysentery if residues are left on cooking or eating utensils, some attract animals and insects, and some are not biodegradable, so harm the environment.

2.

Aesthetics

Yes, as everyone knows, meditation and water are wedded forever.

—H. Melville, *Moby Dick*

TASTE AND ODOR

39. *"Why does my drinking water taste or smell 'funny,' and will this smelly water make me sick?"*

The three most common reasons for bad tasting or smelling water are:

• A funny taste can come from the chlorine that is added to the water to kill germs.

• A rotten-egg odor in some groundwater is caused by a nontoxic (in small amounts), smelly chemical—hydrogen sulfide— dissolved in the water.

• As algae and tiny fungi grow in surface water sources, they give off nontoxic, smelly chemicals that can cause unpleasant tastes in drinking water. Different algae cause different tastes and odors—"grassy," "swampy," and "pigpen," as examples—and the little fungi can cause an "earthy-musty" taste.

None of the contaminants that could affect your health can be tasted in drinking water, but heavily chlorinated water may contain "reaction products." There are no proven incidents of the chemicals that cause a bad taste in drinking water making people sick, but just to be extra careful, water suppliers are reviewing this possibility. You should report any sudden change in taste or smell in your drinking water to your water supplier.

(See Questions 2, 6, 28, 29, and 51 for related information.)

40. *"What can I do if my drinking water tastes 'funny'?"*

Four suggestions are:

• Store some drinking water in a closed glass container in the refrigerator (warm drinking water has more taste than cold drinking water). Although some plastic bottles are okay for storing drinking water in the refrigerator, some types of plastic will cause a taste in water. If you are having trouble, use a different kind of plastic.

• Use an electric mixer or blender to beat or blend the drinking water for five minutes. This mixing will remove some of the bad taste but not all of it. Remember that to be smelled, the chemicals that cause the smell must leave the water, get into the air, and enter your nose. When you beat or blend the water, you hasten the chemicals leaving the water and get rid of some of the odor-causing chemicals prior to drinking the water. Then there are fewer chemicals to smell when you do drink.

• Some people object to the chlorine taste of their drinking water. Boiling tap water for five minutes should remove most of the disinfectant, if not all of it. Of course, some of the minerals in the water will be concentrated a little by the boiling, but this should not be a problem in most cases. After the water cools, refrigerate it. Remember that once the disinfectant is removed, the water must be treated like any other food. Keep it covered and use it as quickly as possible.

• Adding one or two teaspoons of lemon juice to refrigerated drinking water may result in a pleasant-tasting drink.

If the problem is the rotten-egg odor, you may wish to consider a piece of home treatment equipment that will remove hydrogen sulfide, a nontoxic (in small amounts), but offensive chemical that causes this problem.

If you have a water softener (See Question 55) that is on both the hot and cold water, chlorine will react with the softening materials inside the softener, and the chlorine will be removed. Thus, you may not have a chlorine taste, even though chlorine is added by the water supplier.

You should report any unusual taste or odor to your water supplier.

(See Questions 6, 28, and 51 for related information.)

APPEARANCE

41. *"Drinking water often looks cloudy when first taken from a faucet, and then it clears up. Why is that?"*

The cloudy water is caused by tiny air bubbles in the water similar to the gas bubbles in beer and soda pop. After a little while, the bubbles rise to the top and are gone. This type of cloudiness occurs more often in the winter, when the drinking water is cold.

42. *"My drinking water is reddish or brown. What causes this?"*

First, this reddish brown color is nontoxic, but it is not harmless. It can stain clothing in the wash, and it looks bad.

The three possible causes are:

• Your drinking water may contain a brown chemical that results from the source water flowing over tree leaves, similar to the way water changes color after tea leaves are added to it. This color must be removed by the treatment plant; you can't do much about it yourself.

• Iron, which sometimes occurs in nature, may be dissolved in your drinking water. When iron is dissolved in groundwater, it is colorless, but when it combines with air as you take water from your faucet, or elsewhere in the system, the iron turns reddish brown. If you notice the water changing from colorless to brown, you may want to consider buying an iron-removal unit for your home.

• Drinking water pipes —in the street, leading to your home, or in your home—may be rusting, creating rusty-brown water. Water causing this type of problem is called **corrosive.** Also, your hot water tank may be rusting. If you are having trouble and your neighbors are not, then your own pipes or water heater probably are rusting. Letting the water run a while will often clear the water up (save the rusty water for plants). When your plumbing is rusting, lead and copper may be getting into your drinking water as well. This is important, so call your local water supplier to discuss this. To avoid problems with lead and copper, by law, all water suppliers will have to make sure that drinking water is not corrosive.

(See Questions 21, 23, 51, and 65 for related information.)

43. *"My drinking water is dark in color, nearly black. What causes this?"*

When manganese, a chemical currently thought to be nontoxic that frequently occurs in nature, dissolves in groundwater, it is colorless. When it combines with the chlorine that is in the water as it comes to your home, it turns black. To prevent "black water" problems, the U.S. Environmental Protection Agency established a recommended limit (not required, just recommended) for manganese in drinking water. If you have blackish water, you may want to consider a filter to remove manganese from your home. You should also report your problem to your water supplier.

(See Question 51 for related information.)

3.

Home Facts

Water, which so many townspeople never think about, having an obedient spring in the kitchen, is really among the most fragile of life's necessities.

—H. V. Morton, *The Waters of Rome*

GENERAL

44. *"How long can I store drinking water?"* Drinking water that is thoroughly disinfected can be stored indefinitely in capped plastic or glass containers that water will not rust, as metal containers may. Be careful to use plastic that will not make the water taste bad—trial and error is best here. Because the taste will become "flat" after extended storage, periodic replacement is recommended. If possible, you should store water in a refrigerator to help prevent bacterial (not germ) growth.

45. *"Is it okay to use hot water from the tap for cooking?"* No. Use cold water. Hot water is more likely to contain rust, copper, and lead from your household plumbing and water heater because these contaminants generally dissolve into hot water from the plumbing faster than into cold water.

While we're on the subject of hot water, here's a good conservation tip: Insulating your hot water pipes will help keep the water in them warm between hot water uses. Thus, after the first use of the day, hot water will come to the tap sooner, conserving water.

(See Questions 21, 23, 42, and 66 and Chapter 4 for related information.)

46. *"What causes the banging or popping noise that some water heaters, radiators, and pipes make?"* Each noise has a different cause. In a water heater, some of the nontoxic minerals in the water form a rough coating on the inside of the heater when the water warms up. When the container walls are rough, air bubbles form before the water boils. These bubbles burst as the water is heated, causing a popping noise. In a smooth-walled container, heated water will not form bubbles until it boils, and boiling does not occur in a hot water heater, so no noises will be heard when a water heater is new. Occasionally flushing the water heater from the bottom will prevent some, but not all, of the coating from forming.

In a home radiator heated with steam, the banging noise is caused by steam bubbles collapsing in water that is pooled in the system.

Pipes make noises for two reasons. First, when you open a hot water tap after water hasn't been used for a while, the pipe will be cold. As the hot water runs through the pipe, the pipe heats up and gets bigger. This will sometimes cause the pipe to creak or make other noises.

The other reason is **water hammer.** When water is running through a pipe fast and the flow is stopped quickly, the water keeps moving for a while, like a train plowing forward during a wreck. The moving water finally bangs against (hammers) the faucet or valve, making a loud noise, like a hammer hitting metal. If you've noticed this problem in your home, it can easily be corrected by simply turning the water off more slowly.

47. *"Why do hot water heaters fail?"* Because of the natural corrosive properties of all waters, holes will eventually rust through a water heater wall. The time it takes for this to happen varies depending on how corrosive your water is. To avoid problems with lead and copper, water suppliers will be required by law to make water less corrosive.

(See Question 42 for related information.)

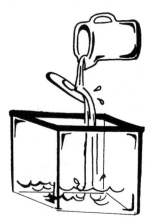

48. *"How should I fill my fish aquarium?"* First, allow at least one gallon of water to run from the tap before using the water to fill the aquarium. This will flush any copper or zinc from copper or galvanized piping in your home; tropical fish are very sensitive to small amounts of copper or zinc in their water. Saving this water for other purposes such as plant watering is a good conservation measure. With a plate in one hand, pour water over the plate into the aquarium, allowing the water to drop about one foot before hitting the plate. This will add air (oxygen) to the water. Let the water sit in the aquarium for an hour or two until it reaches room temperature. Consult your local pet store to learn how to test for and remove any disinfectant in the water. Remove the disinfectant from the water in the aquarium before adding the fish.

(See Question 66 and Chapter 4 for related information.)

Waste Water Treatment Plant

49. *"Where does the water go when it goes down the drain?"* If you are on a sewer system, all of the drains in your house are connected to a single pipe that leads to the street. The pipe in the street collects the wastewater from all the homes in your area and takes it to a larger pipe that collects water from other streets. The wastewater then flows into still bigger pipes that connect various neighborhoods. Think of a large tree with your house at the tip of a branch near the top. Like the tree branches that are bigger nearer the ground, the pipes in the wastewater collection system are larger and contain more water as they near the wastewater treatment plant. Here, the wastewater is treated and cleaned so that it can be put back into the environment without harming anything. A drinking water distribution system (see Chapter 7) looks the same but in this case the drinking water goes *from* the treatment plant to your home.

If you are not connected to a sewer system, the liquid wastes from your home go into a septic tank, where most of the solids settle out. The water then goes into a "leach field," pipes buried in the ground that have holes in the bottom. The water seeps out of these holes and into the ground.

50. *"What can I safely pour down the sink or into the toilet?"*

Before you think about what you can throw away, think about what you are buying. Start by buying environmentally friendly products whenever possible. Next, try to buy just what you'll need so you won't have any or very much left over. Finally, check with your local department of solid waste or similar department for local rules and find out if there are hazardous waste collection days.

If your home is on a sewage system, these liquids can safely be poured down a drain, followed by *plenty* of flush water:

- Aluminum cleaners
- Ammonia-based cleaners
- Drain cleaners
- Window cleaners
- Alcohol-based lotions
- Bathroom cleaners
- Depilatories
- Hair relaxers
- Medicines (expired)
- Permanent lotions
- Toilet bowl cleaners

- Tub and tile cleaners
- Water-based glues
- Paintbrush cleaners with trisodium phosphate
- Lye-based paint strippers

After disposal, be sure to rinse the empty container with water several times before disposal.

If your home has a septic tank, disposal is even more of a problem. Again, checking with your local authorities is a good idea. In general, normal household cleaning products, beauty aids, deodorizers, laundry products, health aids, polishes, soaps, drain cleaners, and expired medicines are acceptable in normal amounts. Of course, the safest course of action is not to put anything in your sink or toilet.

Three good references are:

(1) *Hazardous Wastes in Your Home—What They Are and What to Do with Them,* available from

> Dallas Water Utilities
>
> Dallas, TX 75218 (include a self-addressed-stamped envelope)
>
> (214) 670-3155

(2) *So —Now You Own a Septic System,* WWBRPE20/ Brochure available from the National Small Flows Clearinghouse:

> West Virginia University
>
> P.O. Box 6064
>
> Morgantown, WV 26506-6064
>
> (800) 624-8301

(3) *The Care and Feeding of Your Septic Tank* WWBRPE18/Brochure also available from the National Small Flows Clearinghouse.

In Canada, the local sewer-use bylaw controls disposal in most municipalities.

TREATMENT

51. *"Should I install home water treatment equipment?"*

This is a personal decision. The equipment is not needed to make the water meet federal, state, or provincial drinking water safety standards. In fact, if not properly maintained, the equipment may actually cause water quality problems.

Some people do, however, complain about their drinking water, particularly its taste. If taste is important to you, then you might consider a home treatment unit. Home treatment units, called point-of-use (POU) systems, can be located in several places in the home: countertop, faucet-mounted, under-sink cold tap, under-sink line bypass, or at the point of entry (called POE) into the house.

Treatment units fall into six general categories:

• Particulate filters that remove particles, including black manganese particles, of different sizes.

• Adsorption filters (most of which are not really filters) usually containing activated carbon (sometimes incorrectly called activated charcoal or just charcoal) that remove chlorine, taste and odor, and organic compounds. Some units are capable of removing chlorine-reaction products and some solvents such as cleaning fluid, and pesticides. Microbes do grow in these units (but these usually are not germs), and this fact may be of concern to some. Use of silver-containing activated carbon to prevent the growth of these microbes has not been shown to be uniformly effective or very long lasting. Most adsorption filters remove very little copper and lead. Certain special filters will remove dissolved lead, but unfortunately manufacturers' claims are sometimes not accurate, so be cautious and check their claims with independent organizations, as noted at the end of this answer.

• Oxidation/filtration systems that will change iron (clear water turning red), or hydrogen sulfide (the rotten-egg odor) into a form where these nontoxic, but troublesome chemicals can be filtered out of the water before it comes into your home. These are frequently used by people who have their own source of water, a private well for example.

• Water-softening systems that will trade (exchange) the nontoxic chemicals in your water, which cause "hardness," for other nontoxic chemicals that do not cause hardness. These units have a limited ability to make this change, however and thus must be renewed (regenerated) periodically with salt.

• Reverse osmosis units that remove hardness; chemicals such as nitrates, sodium, dissolved metals and other minerals; and some organic chemicals. Some units are sensitive to chlorine, so a chlorine-removal step usually is included prior to the reverse osmosis unit. Reverse osmosis units do allow some organic chemicals to pass into the treated water, however. Therefore, sometimes these systems are followed by adsorption units to remove these organic compounds. Reverse osmosis units usually produce relatively small volumes of water.

• Distillation units that boil the water and condense the steam to create distilled water remove some organic and inorganic chemicals (hardness, nitrates, chlorine, sodium, dissolved metals, and so forth). However, some organic chemicals may pass through the units with the steam and contaminate the distilled water unless they are specifically designed to avoid this problem.

All of these units require maintenance, should be bought from a reputable dealer, and should be tested and validated against accepted performance standards like those used by the National Sanitation Foundation International (NSF International) and the Water Quality Association (WQA). You should investigate all claims made for any unit. A 1991 study by the U.S. General Accounting Office (GAO) reported that some companies selling these units make fraudulent claims, without regard to the public health risk.

Remember that if the treatment equipment removes the disinfectant present in your tap water, the treated water must be handled like any other food to prevent contamination. It should be refrigerated, kept in a closed container, and used as quickly as possible.

(See Questions 19, 24, 40, 42, 43, 54, 55, 61, 111, and Appendix A for related information.)

52. *"I bought a water filter for my house, and after six months when I went to change it, the filter was covered with gunk. Is my drinking water really okay with all that stuff in it?"*

It is hard to imagine how much water went through the filter in six months to produce that layer of "gunk," but let's do a little figuring. Suppose each eight ounces (equivalent to a glass) of water has 10 particles in it (not much) that can be removed by your filter. This makes 160 particles in a gallon. An average family of four uses about 200 gallons per day, which is a little under 40,000 gallons in six months. This means that your filter had caught almost 6.5 *million* particles by the time you changed it, surely enough to make an impressive-looking film on your filter. So the answer to your question is, yes, the water is okay, and probably has very few particles in each glass of water, too few to be of any harm to you—even if you hadn't used the filter.

53. *"When a piece of home water treatment equipment bears a label that says 'Registered by the U.S. Environmental Protection Agency,' does this mean that the EPA has tested the equipment and that it is effective?"*

No. Some pieces of home treatment equipment are registered under the U.S. Environmental Protection Agency's Pesticide Registration Law, and registration merely means that the piece of equipment has been tested to make sure it doesn't give off any contaminants that will hurt the consumer, regardless of whether it works or not. The U.S. government does not test home treatment equipment to see if it works in treating water.

In Canada, neither a testing program nor a registration program is available.

HARD AND SOFT WATER

54. *"What is 'hard' water?"*

"Hardness" in drinking water is caused by two non-toxic chemicals (usually called **minerals**)— calcium and magnesium. If calcium and/or magnesium is present in your water, the water is said to be *hard* because making a lather or suds for washing is *hard* (difficult) to do. Thus, cleaning with hard water is hard/difficult. Water with little calcium or magnesium is called *soft* water. Maybe it should be called easy, the opposite of difficult.

(See Questions 23, 51, and 101 for related information.)

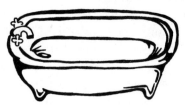

55. *"Should I install a water softener in my home?"* If you are bothered by a sticky, gummy soap curd deposit in your bathtub or by the buildup of white deposits (called **scale**) on your cooking pots and coffee maker, a water softener can help with these problems. Find out how hard your water is, telephone your local drinking water supplier and ask, "What is the hardness of my drinking water?" The higher the hardness number, the more a water softener will help. If it is more than 120 milligrams per liter, abbreviated mg/L (see Question 113 for a definition of mg/L)— sometimes called 120 parts per million or seven grains per gallon— then you might consider a water softener to reduce the formation of scale in your hot water system and to make washing easier.

The water softener replaces the nontoxic "hardness" minerals with sodium or potassium. The amounts of these elements are relatively insignificant in comparison to what you get in food and should not be a problem, unless your doctor has put you on a special restricted diet.

Whether to put the softener on your main water line or just the hot water line is a complicated issue. Softening only the hot water has some cost and environmental advantages related to **regeneration,** which is a process by which the softening materials (called **resins**) inside the softener can be used over and over again.

Water softeners are regenerated with salt. After the salt is used, it goes down the drain and into the environment— so the less salt used the better. Using less salt also saves you money. If you soften only the hot water, the softener needs regeneration less often. Less water going through the unit means less salt being needed. Also, regenerating a softener after a selected *amount* of water has gone through it rather than on a particular schedule is better, as this prevents wasting salt by regenerating too soon or using the softener after it has stopped softening.

Finally, some people think bathing in completely soft water (both hot and cold water softened) is unpleasant—it feels like the soap won't rinse off. You may be surprised to learn, however, that rinsing is actually more complete in soft water than in hard water. Although you can't see it, when you bathe or wash your hair in hard water, some of the same stuff that causes the bathtub ring gets on your body or in your hair. With soft water this material does not form, so rinsing is more complete.

Softening only the hot water has two disadvantages. One, if you wash your clothes in cold water, you won't get the benefit of soft water; however, you can buy products to add to your wash to help if this is a problem. Two, and more important, if your water is very hard—more than twice the numbers mentioned above—when you mix the hot and cold water together, the water will still be hard and you won't see much benefit from the softener.

Concern has been expressed by some whether the installation of a water softener may raise the lead and copper content of drinking water in homes that are experiencing problems. Probably not, but the U.S. Environmental Protection Agency is conducting research to investigate these matters.

(See Questions 21, 23, and 34 for related information.)

56. *"What is that white stuff in my coffeepot and on my shower head and glass shower door? How can I get rid of it?"*

Minerals dissolved in water tend to settle out when water is heated or evaporates. These minerals are white and accumulate in coffeepots and on shower heads and glass shower doors.

To remove these minerals, fill the coffeepot with vinegar and let it sit overnight, or soak the shower head overnight in a plastic bowl filled with vinegar. Slowly adding one tablespoon of muriatic acid to one quart of vinegar will help, but is not necessary. Be careful not to spill this mixture. When you are done, carefully discard the contents of the plastic bowl down a drain, and flush the container and sink drain with plenty of water. NOTE: *Rinse the coffeepot or shower head thoroughly after treatment and before use.* Pouring the excess hot liquid out of your coffeepot when you are finished with it will help somewhat in preventing this problem.

White spots on glass shower doors are difficult to remove with vinegar because the spots dissolve very slowly. A better idea is to prevent the spots from forming by wiping the glass door with a damp sponge or towel after each shower.

NOTE: *Some commercial establishments use untreated water for irrigation to save on tap water. If this is groundwater, it may be high in minerals (treatment beyond that mentioned in Question 93 is needed to get minerals out of the water) and if this water gets on your car, it can leave spots. Vinegar will remove them. Rinsing with good water after using the vinegar is wise.*

57. *"Why does my dishwater leave spots on my glasses?"*

The spots that may appear on glassware after it is washed and air-dried are caused by nontoxic minerals that remain on the glass when the water evaporates. Commercial products are available that allow the water to drain from the glassware more completely. Spots on glass shower doors appear for the same reason.

58. *"What causes the whitish layer on the soil of my potted plants?"*

Drinking water contains many nontoxic chemicals. When the water on your plants evaporates, these chemicals are left behind as a whitish layer. Using distilled water on your plants will avoid this problem. Catching rainwater for watering plants is a good idea, but be sure to cover the water so that mosquito larvae do not grow in it, unless you bring it in after each rain. Also, if you have a dehumidifier, the water that comes out of it is good for plant watering. Distilled water, rainwater, and dehumidifier water will wash minerals out of the soil, however, so use a slow-release balanced fertilizer to replace them.

BOTTLED WATER

59. *"Should I buy bottled water?"*

Remember that the U.S. bottled-water industry is less regulated than municipal drinking water. You don't need to buy bottled water for health reasons if your drinking water meets all of the federal, state, or provincial drinking water standards (ask your local supplier). If you want a drink with a different taste, you can buy bottled water, but it costs about a thousand times more than municipal drinking water.

The U.S. Food and Drug Administration now requires bottled water quality standards to be equal to those of the EPA for tap water, but the quality of the finished product is not government-monitored. Bottlers must test their source water and finished product once a year. Any bottled water that contains contaminants in excess of the allowable level is considered mislabeled unless it has a statement of substandard quality. Although recent tests have not found any lead in dozens of brands of bottled water, studies have shown that microbes may grow in the bottles while on grocers' shelves. Canada does have restrictions on labeling bottled water and has minimal quality requirements covered by the Canadian Food and Drug Act.

Certain bottlers simply fill their bottles with city drinking water, thus producing bottled water that is no different than municipal water, although fifteen states require the source of the water to be on the label if the water is sold in the state where it is bottled.

Bottled water is popular; its use in the United States has doubled in the last six years, and now the flavored, fizzy waters have reached the market. Overall about 10–15 percent of U.S. households drink bottled water regularly. Remember, if you use bottled water, consider it a food and refrigerate it after opening.

NOTE: *Individuals placed on a highly restricted sodium diet should choose a brand of bottled water that contains 0 milligrams (mg.) of sodium in an eight ounce glass of water. Caution: Some bottles labeled sodium-free contain some sodium, maybe too much for those on a highly restricted sodium diet. Check the label carefully on any bottle of water you buy to find out the sodium content of that particular brand, regardless of the general labeling.*

(See Question 111 for related information.)

60. *"What do the various labels on bottled water mean?"*

• **Sparkling water** is water from any source that was made bubbly by adding the gas carbon dioxide from an outside source.

• **Seltzer** is virtually the same as sparkling water, but the source is almost always tap water.

• **Club soda** is similar to seltzer, except that mineral salts have been added. It typically has more sodium than seltzers and sparkling waters.

• **Natural sparkling water** has enough natural carbon dioxide to be bubbly without any other chemicals being added.

• **Sparkling natural water** is usually spring water that has had carbon dioxide gas added.

• **Spring water** comes from a spring, water flowing

out of the ground, with no minerals added or removed.

• **Mineral water** is water containing more than 500 milligrams in each liter of dissolved inorganic chemicals (minerals) such as calcium, sodium, chloride, and sulfate. (These minerals are believed by some people to be of some health benefit, although there is no scientific evidence to support such claims.)

• **Natural water** has no minerals added or removed.

• **Purified water** has all of the minerals and chemicals removed by many treatment steps.

• **Distilled water** is made by boiling water, then catching the steam and cooling it down into water.

• **Still water** is water without gas bubbles.

In fifteen states, if the water is bottled in the same state where it is sold, the source must be identified, and twenty-three states have passed laws regulating some aspect of bottled water.

The U.S. Food and Drug Administration (FDA) has proposed new rules that would change the labeling of bottled water. The proposal was published in the *Federal Register* on December 31, 1993, and contained proposed definitions for six types of bottled water: mineral water, artesian water, purified water, spring water, distilled water, and well water. The proposal did not cover carbonated water, soda water, or tonic water, which were considered soft drinks. The public comment period is over and the final rule with definitions is expected sometime in 1995. When you read or hear that the new rules are out, you can get information by calling the FDA at 202-205-4681 and asking for details of the new requirements.

61. *"Is dis-tilled water the 'perfect' drinking water?"*

No, for the following reasons:
- It is too expensive.
- It is missing several minerals that are in regular drinking water, minerals that some people believe are beneficial to health.
- It has a taste many describe as flat and unappealing.
- There is no guarantee that it is free from germs.
- Distilled water might be contaminated with organic chemicals. For example, if the distilled water is made by heating water containing contaminants like chloroform and cleaning fluid (solvents), some of these contaminants could be in the steam when the water boils. When the steam is caught and cooled to create the distilled water, it would contain these contaminants.

Distilled water is handy around the home, however, for use in steam irons and car batteries and for watering plants.

(See Questions 19, 51, and 58 for related information.)

62. *"Should I buy drinking water from a vending machine?"*

Buying water from a vending machine is unnecessary if your water meets all of the federal, state, and provincial requirements. The treatment of vending machine water is based on sound scientific principles. The problem is you don't know how often the machines are checked or how well they are maintained. Thus, because you can't tell how well a particular machine is maintained, a definite answer to this question is not possible.

(See Question 111 for related information.)

COST

63. *"What is the cost of the water I use in my home?"* Water delivered to a home is sold using three common units of measure in various parts of the United States: 1,000 gallons, 100 cubic feet (750 gallons), and one acre-foot (327,000 gallons). Prices vary greatly around the United States, but a typical cost is about $2.00 for 1,000 gallons, which is equivalent to $1.50 for 100 cubic feet or $654.00 for one acre-foot. At this price, you get five gallons of tap water for a penny. An average cost for water supplied to a home in Canada is about $2.00 (Canadian) for 1,000 imperial gallons.

One thousand gallons of water would serve one consumer for about twenty days, so tap water is not very expensive. Of the amount charged for 1,000 gallons, about $0.30–$0.40 is for treatment; the rest is for paying the mortgage on the treatment plant and the pipes in the street, the salaries of the employees who work for the drinking water utility, and some profit for privately owned water companies.

You can figure the cost of water in your area by looking at your water bill and dividing the total cost for water by the total amount of water used (just use the water part of the bill if other costs are included). In general, in the United States we spend about

0.5 percent of our income on both drinking water and wastewater disposal.

(See Questions 92 and 118 for related information.)

64. *"How does a water company know how much water I use in my home?"*

Most households have a water meter that measures the amount of water used. One notable exception is in New York City, where many households are charged the same cost (called a flat rate) each month. For those communities with water meters, a person from the water utility reads the meter on a regular schedule. The previous reading is subtracted from the current reading to determine the amount of water actually used.

NOTE: *New York City now (1994) has about one-third of its buildings metered.*

65. *"How does the water company know that my water meter is correct?"*

Most water companies have programs to routinely test water meters on a rotating basis to make sure the meters are accurate. Of course, if your recorded water use changes suddenly for no obvious reason (more people in the home, away for a long trip, or heavy lawn watering), report this to your water supplier so it can be investigated. In most instances, when a water meter is wrong, it reads low. As a good citizen, you should report this to your water supplier just as you would when you think your meter might be reading high.

66. *"We had a conservation drive in our area, and everyone cooperated. Then our water rates went up. Why?"*

Water suppliers have fixed costs—salaries, mortgage payments, and so forth. They must collect this money regardless of water use, so when water volume goes down because of conservation by the public, the cost of each gallon of water used sometimes is raised to provide the water supplier with the money it needs to operate.

(See Chapter 4 for related information.)

4.

Conservation

To take anything for granted, is in a real sense, to neglect it and that is how most of us treat water.

—Robert Raikes, *Water, Weather, and Prehistory*

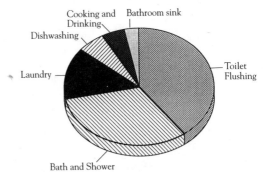

Cooking and Drinking · Bathroom sink · Dishwashing · Laundry · Toilet Flushing · Bath and Shower

67. *"What activity in my home uses the most water?"* Toilet flushing is by far the largest single use of water in a home. Most toilets use from four to six gallons of water for each flush. Canadian flush toilets use about four to six imperial gallons. On the average, a dishwasher uses about 50 percent *less* water than the amount used when you wash and rinse dishes by hand if the dishes are not pre-rinsed and if only full loads are washed in the dishwasher.

Without counting lawn watering, typical percentages of water use for a family of four are:

Toilet flushing	40%
Bath and shower	32%
Laundry	14%

Dishwashing	6%
Cooking and drinking	5%
Bathroom sink	3%

In the United States, the National Energy Act of 1992 requires low-volume toilets in new construction or as replacements in existing homes after January 1, 1994. Businesses must comply by 1997. Ultra-low-flow (ULF) toilets are available, which use only 1.5 to 1.6 gallons for each flush. Low volume toilets are not required in Canada, but water-efficiency plans are in place in many provinces. Plans for new construction are reviewed by appropriate officials in the government.

(See Questions 66 and 118 for related information.)

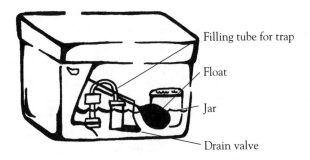

Filling tube for trap

Float

Jar

Drain valve

68. *"Some people say I should put a brick in my toilet tank to save water. How does that save water, and is this a good idea?"*

Toilet flushing does use a lot of water, and putting something in the toilet tank that takes up space means that less water will be used each time the tank refills after a flush, but putting a brick in your toilet tank is not a good idea. A brick tends to crumble and might damage the toilet's flushing mechanism. A glass jar, a plastic bag, or a jug filled with water will work, however. Because some toilets require a certain volume of water to work right, be sure to test the toilet to make sure it's still flushing well after any changes. NOTE: *Never use your toilet as a trash can. Using several gallons of water to get rid of a tissue or a cigarette is very wasteful.*

Also remember that toilet tanks can leak. To check, put a few drops of food coloring in the tank, wait about fifteen minutes, and look in the bowl. If the food coloring shows up there, the tank is leaking and should be fixed. Toilets should be checked for leaks every year. Many large utilities give away conservation kits with food coloring tablets, flow restrictors, and plastic bags to fill with water and put in toilet tanks.

(See Question 66 for related information.)

69. *"I heard that it's a good idea to control the flow of water from my shower head. How do I measure how fast my shower is using water?"*

You need two things: a bucket and a watch that can time seconds. The bucket needs to have a one-gallon mark on it. If it doesn't, add a gallon of water and mark the level.

Set the shower flow just as you would when showering. Put the empty bucket under the showerhead to catch all the water and hold it there for twenty-four seconds (having someone else hold the watch probably will help make this easier). The bucket will weigh eight to ten pounds (10 to 12 pounds in Canada) after the twenty-four seconds, so be prepared.

If the water is near the one-gallon mark, your showerhead is flowing at the recommended amount. If the level is way over the one-gallon mark, you should consider a new low-flow showerhead (flow restrictors often produce a weak spray) to conserve water. The National Energy Act of 1992 requires low-flow showerheads (less than 2.5 gallons each minute) in any new construction and replacements after January 1, 1994.

(See Question 66 for related information.)

70. *"Why are there aerators on home water faucets?"*

When mixed with water, tiny air bubbles from the aerator prevent the water from splashing too much. Because the water flow is less, often half the regular flow, aerators also help conserve water.

(See Question 66 for related information.)

71. *"I leave the water running while I'm brushing my teeth. Does that waste much water?"*

Leaving the water running is a bad habit; about five to six gallons of water go down the drain needlessly every time you brush. Turning off the water when you are not using it will save water and save you some money.

Another way many people unthinkingly waste water is while they are waiting for the hot water to come to a shower, tub, or sink. Catching this water to use for plant watering is a good conservation tip.

(See Question 66 for related information.)

72. *"Many water quality problems in the home — lead, red water, sand in the system, and so forth — are cured by flushing the system. But isn't that a waste of water?"*

Flushing does take water, but you can avoid losing this water by catching it in a container and using it for plant and garden watering. Even if you don't do this, strictly speaking the flush water is not wasted. A true waste of water is a use that gives no benefit, like leaving the water running while you brush your teeth, setting your lawn sprinkler so the water lands on your driveway or street, or flushing the toilet to get rid of a tissue. Flush water does provide a benefit if it keeps lead or rust out of your water or brings hot water to your tub. So, do try to use your flush water, but if you can't, don't feel too bad. This water has served a useful purpose.

73. *"My water faucet drips a little; should I bother to fix it?"*

Yes. Drips waste a precious product, and this waste should be stopped, even though the dripping water may not register on your water meter. To find out how much water you're wasting, put an eight-ounce measuring cup (or anything that will let you measure eight ounces) under the drip and find out how many minutes it takes to fill it up. Divide the filling time into 90 (90 ÷ minutes to fill) to get the gallons of water wasted each day.

As an example, if you have a faucet that dripped sixty times a minute (once each second) this adds up to over 3 gallons each day or 1,225 gallons each year, enough to fill more than twenty-two 55-gallon drums, just from one dripping faucet. This leak would fill the eight-ounce measuring cup in less than thirty minutes.

74. *"How should I water my lawn to avoid wasting water?"*

Water your lawn for long periods a couple of times each week, rather than every day. This allows deep penetration of the water. An inch a week is a good rule of thumb, but this varies for different grasses and different parts of the country. Check with your local garden store. If you want to find out exactly how long to water, put some large jars or cans (peanut butter jars will work) around your lawn and see how long you have to run your sprinkler to fill the jars with the right amount of water.

Water early in the morning to avoid excessive evaporation; it is usually less windy then, too, and the water pressure is usually higher. Night watering may promote lawn disease. Use a sprinkler that makes large drops, because small drops evaporate faster. Watering your lawn with a handheld hose is a waste of both your time and your water, although it might be okay for a small garden.

Try to avoid watering paved areas, and don't use your hose to wash sidewalks or driveways. Both of these practices waste a lot of water.

Plant watering can be reduced by selecting xeriscape (ZEER·uh·scape, which means low-water-demanding) plants or native plants, which provide an attractive landscape without high water use. Two good references are:

1) *Xeriscape Gardening,* by Welsh, Ellefson, and Stephens (1992)

Macmillan Publishing Co.
100 Front Street
Riverside, NJ 08075
(800) 428-5331; and

2) *Xeriscape Programs for Water Utilities* (This includes good ideas for homeowners, too.)

American Water Works Association
(800) 926-7337.

Remember, pets need water in the summer just as your lawn and garden do. If you keep a pet out-of-doors, provide plenty of water in a shady area. Secure the water bowl so that it will not spill. Ice cubes added from time to time to keep the water cool will really help your pet.

(See Questions 11 and 66 for related information.)

75. *"Why do we still have a water shortage when it's been raining at my house?"*

Your drinking water may come from far away, so even if it's raining at your house, it may not be raining where the water supplier collects its water. If this happens, the rain in your area doesn't help the water shortage, but it usually does lower the demand for water while it is raining because people stop watering lawns and gardens and washing their cars.

(See Questions 79 and 80 for further information.)

76. *"During times of water shortages, shouldn't decorative fountains be turned off?"*

In most cases, fountain water is recirculated (used over and over) and is not wasted. If water losses from evaporation are high, however, fountains should be turned off.

77. *"During times of water shortage, does not serving water to restaurant customers really help?"*

Skipping water in restaurants serves as a good reminder to everyone about the importance of saving water, but the actual volume of water saved is small. However, the water that is used to wash the water glasses is also saved, and this is usually more than the drinking water that would normally be served by glass to customers. By comparison, each flush of a toilet uses the equivalent of about eighty glasses of drinking water.

Health experts emphasize the importance of drinking at least six to eight glasses of water each day (remember you drink water in many forms—in juices, milk, pop, coffee, tea, etc.), so if you want water to drink, ask for it. Skip it if you are just going to let the glass sit on the table while you drink something else.

A good reference on conservation is: *A Consumer's Guide to Water Conservation: Dozens of Ways to Save Water, the Environment, and a Lot of Money*, published by the American Water Works Association. Call (800) 926-7337, and ask for item No. 10063. You could also call WaterWiser—The Water Efficiency Clearinghouse at (800) 559-9855.

(See Questions 24, 45, 48, 66, and 90 for more comments about conservation.)

5.

Sources

Water is more precious than gold and more explosive than dynamite.

—E. K. McQuery

GENERAL

78. *"Where does my drinking water come from?"*

There are two major sources of drinking water: surface water and groundwater. Surface water comes from lakes, reservoirs, and rivers. Groundwater comes from wells that the water supplier drills into aquifers. An aquifer is an underground geologic formation through which water flows slowly. Some wells are shallow—50 to 100 feet deep; others are deep—1,500 to 2,000 feet.

Springs are another source of water. Springs begin underground as groundwater. When the water is pushed to the surface and flows out of the ground naturally, it becomes a spring. The water then may flow over the surface of the ground as surface water.

Most large cities in the United States —New York, Los Angeles, Chicago, Philadelphia, Boston, Saint Louis, New Orleans, Seattle, Denver, and part of Houston—to name a few, use surface water. The larger cities in Canada, including Montreal, Toronto, Edmonton, and Vancouver, also use surface water.

Most small towns and some large cities — including Miami, Tucson, part of Houston, and parts of

Cincinnati—use groundwater. Tucson and Houston are planning to stop using groundwater, however. A large Canadian city that uses groundwater is Kitchener–Waterloo, Ontario. About 80 million people in the United States use groundwater supplied through individual wells and municipal groundwater systems. About 2 million people in Canada are supplied by municipal groundwater systems.

Some water suppliers buy treated water from others (wholesalers) and then provide water to their customers, often without further treatment.

Your local water utility can tell you the specific source of your drinking water.

79. *"Are we running out of water?"* Globally we have sufficient fresh water to satisfy the need for drinking water, but frequently it is not located where the high-use areas are. Thus, localized water shortages occur. Furthermore, **droughts** (below-normal rainfall), often lasting several years, worsen water shortages in some areas.

80. *"How does nature recycle water?"* The **water cycle** keeps the amount of total water on the globe constant. Water from oceans, lakes, rivers, ponds, puddles, and other water surfaces evaporates to become clouds. The clouds make rain, snow, or sleet that falls to earth to make rivers and streams, some of which seep into the ground to form groundwater. All of this water flows to the ocean to start the cycle over again. Before returning to the ocean, some of this water is taken for drinking water and then is discharged as wastewater. The cycle is never-ending.

81. *"When I see pictures of the earth from outer space, it looks like it's mostly covered with water. Is that right, and how much of this water is drinkable?"*

You're right. Between 70 and 80 percent of the earth is covered with water, but less than one percent of this visible (surface) water can be made into drinking water with proper treatment. Remember, however, that great quantities of water are available underground that cannot be seen from space. This water is called groundwater. In the United States alone there is an estimated 265 billion gallons of freshwater used for all purposes every day from surface water and 73 billion gallons used from groundwater. So you can see how important this "invisible" groundwater is.

Of all the water in the world, 97 percent is in the oceans, 2 percent is in icecaps and glaciers, 0.6 percent is underground, 0.3 percent is in the atmosphere, and 0.1 percent is in rivers, lakes, and reservoirs.

82. *"Many areas near the ocean do not have large supplies of fresh water. Why can't ocean water be treated to make drinking water?"*

Ocean water can be treated, but the process is expensive. On the other hand, so is the economic cost of not having enough water. The cost of converting salt water to drinking water has been estimated at five to seven dollars for each one thousand gallons instead of the thirty to forty cents for each thousand gallons for the treatment described in Question 93. Ocean water contains so much salt that at least 99.2 percent of the salt would have to be removed to avoid a salty taste in drinking water.

(See Question 63 for related information.)

83. *"Can wastewater be treated to make it into drinking water?"*

This is not done at the present time, although a large test has been completed in Denver, Colorado, to study the possibility. This test showed that good quality drinking water could be made from wastewater, but so far water shortages have not been so severe that this measure has been needed. Of course, nature reuses water through the water cycle.

To save water in some areas of the United States, treated wastewater is used to irrigate golf courses and landscaped public areas, although this practice is not without controversy. This irrigation practice is not promoted in Canada.

QUALITY

84. *"Which is more polluted, groundwater or surface water?"*

It depends on what you call pollution. Because surface water can be contaminated by municipal sewage, industrial discharges, transportation accidents, and rainfall runoff, it contains many pollutants but not much of any one chemical. Groundwater, on the other hand, may contain pollutants such as arsenic, nitrates, radioactive materials, and high (compared with surface water) amounts of a few organic chemicals such as cleaning fluid. Therefore, both may be polluted, but in different ways. Another difference is that the degree of pollution may change rapidly in surface waters, while pollution levels change very slowly in groundwaters. Your water supplier can tell you what contaminants it has found in its source water, but it tests the quality of its treated water more than its source water.

85. *"In towns and cities, what is the major cause of pollution of drinking water sources?"*

The major source of pollution is rainwater that flows into street catch basins (called **urban runoff** or **storm-water runoff**). While this rainwater alone is not necessarily harmful, it frequently carries untreated waste products from our streets and yards directly into rivers, streams, and lakes (drinking water sources). In 1989, for example, Americans dumped 365 million gallons of motor oil, which found its way into our drinking water sources.

86. *"Why isn't urban runoff usually treated before being discharged into drinking water sources?"*

Because runoff from rainfall occurs only when it rains, it doesn't make sense to build special treatment processes for those times when it isn't raining. As an analogy, having extra servers at a restaurant all day to avoid any delays at lunch time is not practical, as they would be idle at other times of the day. Chicago has one possible solution—capturing and holding the runoff during storms and then pumping it slowly and steadily to the wastewater plant for treatment prior to discharge. Other cities use ponds to hold the runoff for a while so that its quality can improve by settling out some contaminants before discharge. Because runoff is an important source of pollution, legislation that deals with storm-water runoff is changing the way it must be treated, in spite of the difficulties.

87. *"Does acid rain affect water supplies?"*

Some air pollutants do dissolve in raindrops and make them **acidic,** like lemon juice, but the effect of this acid rain on water supplies is small. Certain lakes in the northeastern United States and in certain regions of Canada seem to be a little more acid than they were years ago, but the changes are minor and current rules require water suppliers to remove any acidity before the water goes to the consumer. Groundwater usually is not affected because the alkaline materials in soils (like the chemicals in antacid tables) react with the acid rain to neutralize it before it reaches the groundwater. An exception to this rule occurs in northern Ontario, Canada, where the groundwater is near the surface. In that location, there is not enough soil to neutralize the acid rain before it reaches the groundwater. Even though the groundwater in this area is a little acid, most of the utilities here use surface water, which is fine. The few municipalities that do use groundwater add chemicals to react with the acid and destroy it to avoid acid (corrosive) water. Most of the groundwater use in the area is by individuals with private wells, and most of them do nothing to treat the water.

(See Questions 21, 23, 42, 47, and 101 for related information.)

88. *"I read about the problem of oil spills. Do they pollute drinking water sources?"*

Although oil spilled in the oceans is bad for the environment, it is not a danger to drinking water sources. However, ship and barge accidents can contaminate surface water sources (rivers and lakes). Many highways and railroad tracks pass over drinking water sources, creating a potential for contamination if a truck or freight-train accident occurs. A motor vehicle accident or poor disposal of oil from your car can cause oil pollution. Drinking water contaminated with even a little bit of oil has such a bad taste that most people regard it as undrinkable.

Although groundwater sources are not directly affected by most of these types of accidents, unless they occur in the **recharge area** (where water seeps downward to add water to the underground aquifer), major oil spills can cause nearly irreversible damage to groundwater.

89. *"How can I help prevent pollution of drinking water sources?"*

Properly dispose of the chemicals you use in your home. Every chemical you buy has the potential of polluting the environment if disposed of improperly. Try to buy environmentally acceptable alternative products, and, to minimize waste, buy only what you can use. Many larger cities have a hazardous waste disposal department. Check with it if you have disposal questions. If you change the oil in your car yourself, find out from your city, state, or provincial environmental agency how to properly dispose of the used oil.

Remember, if your home is served by a sewage system, your drain is an entrance to your wastewater disposal system and eventually to a drinking water source. Discharges from septic tank drain fields may pollute groundwaters. Treat your wastewater system with respect.

(See Questions 22 and 50 for related information.)

90. *"Why does my water sometimes have sand in it?"*

Routine cleaning of pipes that carry drinking water can stir up material that has settled to the bottom of the pipes. This can give your water a temporary sandy appearance. Some wells have specially designed screens (like window screens) to hold back the sand, and a break in this screen is another possible cause of sandy water. Small quantities of sand may pass through a well screen, even if it is not broken. The best way to solve this problem is to verify with your water supplier that there is no break in the system, and if there is none, flush your home pipes by running water for a while through your largest faucet, probably in the bathtub. Saving this water for other uses is a good conservation measure. Some particles that look like sand may actually result from the corrosion of galvanized pipes in your household plumbing.

(See Questions 23, 42, 47, and 66 and Chapter 4 for related information.)

6.

Suppliers

Men work on earth at many things;
Some till the soil, a few are kings;
But the noblest job beneath the sun
Is making Running Water *run.*

—John L. Ford, *Water and Wastewater Engineering*

91. *"How many drinking water suppliers are there in the United States and Canada?"* There are approximately 200,000 community and non-community drinking water suppliers in the United States. The U.S. Safe Drinking Water Act (the federal law regulating drinking water) defines a **community** water supplier as a utility that provides drinking water to 25 people or more all the time. There are just under 60,000 community water suppliers in the United States. Most are small; about 63 percent are in towns with 500 people or fewer. About 250 community suppliers serve populations of 100,000 or more—that is, about 110 million Americans in all. In addition, there are about 140,000 **non-community** drinking water suppliers —motels, remote restaurants, and similar establishments that serve the traveling public. While they too may serve many people, they don't serve them on an ongoing basis. All of these 200,000 drinking water suppliers must meet some or all of the federal drinking water regulations. Because you don't stay in one place for very long when you are traveling, non-community supplies don't have to meet as many federal regulations as does your home supply where you drink the water almost all of the time.

In the United States, about 13 million people (5 percent of the population) are supplied water by their own private wells. These wells are not federally regulated under the Safe Drinking Water Act.

In Canada, a municipal supply is defined as one serving five households or more. There are about 5,000 municipal supplies, with about 60 percent serving small communities. In addition, there are about 50,000 private communal supplies that serve the traveling public and small permanent facilities. About 4 million Canadians obtain water from their own private wells.

(See Question 109 for related information.)

92. *"Are all drinking water utilities owned by cities and towns?"*   No. In the United States, about 56 percent of drinking water suppliers are privately owned, just like any other company. The amount these companies charge their customers for drinking water is controlled by state public utilities commissions. Many of these companies are listed on the New York Stock Exchange or other exchanges, and the public may purchase shares. In Canada, almost all of the municipal supplies are publicly owned, although recently at least one utility—in Alberta, Canada—has become privately owned.

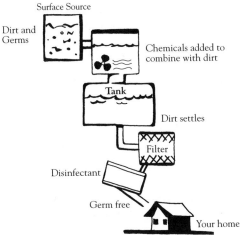

Drinking Water Treatment Plant

93. *"How is my drinking water treated?"*

Currently in the United States about 50 percent of groundwater supplies are distributed untreated. In the near future, except in special cases, the government will require that at least disinfection, which is performed to kill germs, be done.

Most surface waters first are treated with chemicals that combine with dirt particles. The dirt then can be settled and filtered out of the water, making it clear. Filtering is important because, besides making the water clear, it removes some germs that are very difficult to kill. Finally, the water is disinfected to kill the remaining germs. Thus, tap water is a manufactured product, starting with a raw material (surface water) and processing it to turn it into a finished product, your drinking water. Groundwater is usually clear when it is pumped out of the ground; thus, it can be disinfected without prior treatment. Occasionally additional treatment is needed to solve special problems. The treatment described above does not remove dissolved toxic chemicals, so it is used only when they are not present, the most common case.

In March, 1994, a report entitled "Victorian Water

Treatment Enters the 21st Century" was released to the press. One point made in this report was that "obsolete" treatment techniques were being used in this country. Although it is true that the treatment methods described above are the same ones that were in use in the early 1900s, the improvements that have been made in them over the years have dramatically improved their performance, yielding a much higher quality drinking water. Cars still have four wheels, but the new models are quite different from a Model T. Additional treatment beyond what is now "conventional" is expected in the future, moreover, as water suppliers make strides to make drinking water even safer than it is today.

Many different chemicals are used by your supplier during the water treatment process. Some of these chemicals are removed along with the pollutants; others remain in the water. The ones left, however, are either nontoxic or their use is strictly limited.

The same treatment situation exists in Canada, but some Canadian provinces require disinfection as the minimum treatment.

(See Questions 12, 18, and 111 for related information.)

94. *"Is it true that some major cities do not filter their drinking water?"*

According to U.S. Environmental Protection Agency regulations, since June 29, 1993, all water suppliers using surface water have been required to use a filtration step in their treatment. The regulation does, however, allow water suppliers not to filter their water, if they can show, by passing a complex set of tests, that their drinking water is safe without filtration. Cities like Boston, New York, Seattle, and Portland are currently discussing their particular conditions with regulatory officials. Filtration has been installed in many locations recently, and is being considered in many others. If you are interested in your local situation, talk to your water supplier.

In Canada a similar situation exists. General policy requires filtration of surface water, but a local supplier that can demonstrate it meets stringent testing, reporting, and quality criteria, need not filter. As in the United States, many localities are assessing the need for filtration.

(See Questions 5, 12, and 78 for related information.)

95. *"I've read all about the problems with my drinking water. Why isn't my water supplier doing something about it?"*

There are several possible answers:

• The utility may be working on the problem but not informing consumers; construction of new facilities takes a long time.

• The utility may want to do something about it but doesn't have the financial resources.

• Because drinking water suppliers are dedicated to providing the best quality drinking water at the least cost to the customer, they may be waiting until all federal regulations are in place before taking action to avoid wasting money on obsolete or unnecessary procedures.

Why don't you call your utility and find out about your specific situation?

(See Chapter 8 on federal regulations for related information.)

96. *"My drinking water is not acceptable. Whom do I complain to?"*

Call your local drinking water supplier and discuss your problem. Your supplier will probably send a representative to your home to help you or to explain what is causing the problem and what the supplier intends to do about it.

97. *"What should I do to help my drinking water supplier improve my drinking water quality?"*

• Call your local drinking water supplier and ask what the major needs are and how you can help.

• Support governmental efforts, such as increases in water rates from your water supplier to improve service, local taxation and bond issues to improve drinking water quality, and similar efforts.

• Write to your state, provincial, or federal legislators urging them to increase funding for support of legislation protecting drinking water quality.

• Discuss these issues with your friends and associates and get their support as well.

98. *"How does a water supplier prepare for a possible natural disaster like a hurricane?"*

If the water supplier has some warning, the supplier will make sure that all necessary chemicals and supplies are available, that the emergency power systems are well supplied with fuel, and that all water storage tanks and basins are filled. Water suppliers have contingency plans to make sure that a continuous supply of drinking water will be available under almost any circumstance.

Many water plants that are built in a flood plain are diked to avoid being flooded. The extraordinary floods of 1993 in the midwestern United States and in 1994 in southern Georgia were so high, however, that the dikes could not protect all of the water treatment plants. After an event like that, it takes a long time to deliver *safe* drinking water to the community again because even after the plant is back in operation, killing *all* of the germs in *all* of the pipes underground is very difficult. The water is not safe to drink until extensive testing proves that all is okay again. You will be informed by the water supplier when you can start drinking the water again.

99. *"Is my drinking water subject to sabotage?"*

Sabotage of a water supply is highly unlikely. Groundwater sources are protected because they are underground. Most treatment plants are staffed around-the-clock, thus providing security. Because the volumes of water treated are generally large, the quantity of a contaminant that would have to be added to pollute a water supply is so great that sabotage is almost impossible.

7.

Distribution

Sub-human primates, like other animals, drink where the water flows.

Only man carries it to where he lives.

— C. S. Coon, *The History of Man*

100. *"Are the pipes that carry drinking water from the treatment plant to my home clean?"*

A well-run water utility will have an ongoing program of flushing and cleaning the distribution pipes to ensure that these pipes are clean. Otherwise, rust and microbes would cling to the pipe walls. Flushing is done by opening fire hydrants and letting the water rush out.

Another way to clean pipes is by forcing a tight-fitting plastic sponge through the pipe using water pressure. The sponge scrapes the pipe walls clean. The dirt then is flushed out a fire hydrant. Similar devices with other designs are also available.

Keeping water pipes clean is a big job, as there are

about one million miles of pipes in the United States and Canada.

101. *"What are asbestos-cement pipes that carry water under the streets? Are they safe?"*

Asbestos-cement pipes are made from cement with asbestos fibers added to make the pipes strong. Most drinking water passes through these pipes without becoming contaminated with asbestos fibers, and so they are safe. Although asbestos has been banned for many uses by the U.S. government because of the health risks caused by breathing asbestos fibers, asbestos-cement pipes are exempted. However, they are not too popular in new construction. Cement-lined iron pipe is the most common type these days.

A few types of drinking water—water that is slightly acid or contains few minerals—tend to dissolve the cement, softening the pipe and releasing the asbestos fibers into the drinking water. Asbestos-cement pipes should not be used to carry these types of drinking water. Because of the U.S. Environmental Protection Agency's lead and copper regulation, water quality must be adjusted to make sure that the water is not corrosive, thus helping prevent fiber release. Remember, if the pipe stays solid and is not softened by the water flowing through it, the fibers are so tightly bound in the pipe material that they will not be released and the pipe is safe.

Additionally, the U.S. Environmental Protection Agency limits the number of asbestos fibers permitted in drinking water. This is important because studies have shown that ultrasonic humidifiers using water that contains asbestos fibers may put fibers into the air where they might be dangerous because they are inhaled. Asbestos fibers are much more dangerous when inhaled than when they are swallowed.

Asbestos fibers in drinking water are not regulated in Canada, and except for avoiding slightly acid waters, asbestos-cement pipe can be used.

To learn about water conditions in your area and to find out if asbestos-cement pipes are used, call your water company.

(See Question 54 for related information.)

102. *"We don't use much water for drinking. Why does all the rest need to be treated so extensively? This seems unnecessarily expensive."*

Actually the cost of water *treatment* is a small part of your water bill (only about $0.45 to $0.60 each month for each person living in your house), but that is not the real answer. A new town could be developed in which two pipes come into your home from the street (a **dual distribution system**), one small pipe for drinking water and a larger pipe for all of the other uses for water (toilet flushing, lawn watering, and so forth). To take out all of the pipes and install such a system in existing towns and cities would cost far too much.

In any case, the water provided for purposes other than drinking would still need to be free of germs and any chemicals that would stain laundry or form deposits on pipes. Thus, even this water would require some treatment, making the dual distribution system idea even less attractive.

(See Question 63 for related information.)

103. *"How does a water company detect a major leak in the distribution piping system?"*

A major leak can be detected by

• Visual detection (water on the ground) by water company employees who work in the field;

• A loss in pressure that can be detected by the water company and customers;

• Reports by public-minded citizens.

Once a leak is suspected, its precise location is determined by water utility personnel. Sensitive listening devices are used to detect the sound of the leaking water underground.

Stopping leaks is important to a water supplier because leaks waste water, adding cost to both the water supplier and you. The water supplier doesn't get paid for the water that is lost to leaks but may pass its cost along to the customers. The national average for water lost from leaks is 15 percent, although most suppliers try to keep such losses to around 10 percent.

Any leakage that occurs within the boundary of your property after the water meter is your responsibility and must be repaired at your own expense. Prompt repair is to your benefit, because as long as the pipe is leaking, your water bill will be higher.

104. *"If leaks are such a waste of water, why doesn't the water utility just fix them?"* Your water supplier is certainly trying to minimize leaks because they do waste water. Leaks may result from old rusting pipes or from ground movement that causes pipes to break or their joints to crack. In the complex network of pipes necessary to supply water throughout a community, it is almost inevitable that at any one time some leakage will be occurring. Many water departments have special teams to measure leakage, locate and repair leaks, find weak points in the pipe network, and replace rusting pipes. Leaks also can be controlled, but not eliminated, by the supplier's avoiding unnecessarily high water pressure.

105. *"Fixing a broken water pipe looks like a dirty job. How is the inside of the pipe cleaned afterwards?"*

After the work is done, the pipe is filled with water containing a large amount of chlorine. Holding this water in the pipe for a time kills all the germs.

This is not the end of the story, however. The next problem is how to dispose of all this water that contains so much chlorine. State, provincial, and federal regulations control its disposal. A chemical must be added to react with the chlorine and destroy it before the water can be flushed out of the pipe and discharged, or the highly chlorinated water must be discharged to an area where it will not have an impact on the environment.

106. *"What are the causes of low water pressure, and should low water pressure concern me?"*

Temporary low pressure can be caused by heavy water use in your area—lawn watering, a water main break, fighting a nearby fire, and so on. Permanent low pressure could be caused by the location of your home—on a hill or far from the pumping plant— or your home may be served by pipes that are too small.

Low pressure is more than just a nuisance. The water system depends on pressure to keep out any contamination. If the pressure drops, the possibility of pollution entering the drinking water increases. You should report any permanent drop in water pressure to your water company.

Many areas have minimum standards for pressure. For

example, 20 pounds per square inch (psi) when water use is at a maximum is a common standard (car tires often use 30 to 32 psi of air). Most systems have pressures three to four times the minimum.

You can tell you may have low pressure if flows from your faucets at home are much lower than elsewhere in your area—at work, in a restaurant wash room, or in a friend's home elsewhere in the city, for example. The only way to cure low pressure is to have the supplier change the system, adding more pumps or bigger lines, but because low pressure is a possible health hazard, keeping the pressure up is important.

You may be surprised to learn that you can also have too much pressure. Some homes need pressure regulators to avoid damaging household plumbing from very high water pressures.

107. *"What are cross-connections, and why are they a problem?"*

A cross-connection is a connection between a drinking water pipe and a polluted source. Here's a common example. You're going to spray weed killer on your lawn. You hook up your hose to the sprayer that contains the weed killer. If the water pressure drops at the same time you turn on the hose, the chemical in the sprayer may be sucked back into the drinking water pipes through the hose. This would seriously pollute the drinking water system. This problem can be prevented by using an attachment on your hose called a **back-flow prevention device**. This is a way for consumers to help protect their water system.

Most water suppliers have cross-connection control programs, particularly in major cities. Their distribution systems are so complex that tracking down cross-connections is a never-ending job. Removing cross-connections is vital, however, if drinking water quality is to be protected.

108. *"Why is some drinking water stored in large tanks high above the ground?"*

Two reasons. One, this type of storage ensures that water pressure and water volume are sufficient to fight fires, even if the electricity that runs the water pumps is off. The second reason is to provide an extra source of drinking water during the day when water use is high. The tanks are refilled at night when drinking water use is low.

8.

Regulations and Testing

It was Emperor Nero's invention to boil water, and then enclose it in glass vessels and cool it in the snow. Indeed, it is generally admitted all water is more wholesome boiled.

—John Bostock and H. T. Ripley,
The Natural History of Pliny

FEDERAL REGULATIONS

109. *"What federal legislation protects the quality of drinking water?"* In the United States, the Safe Drinking Water Act (administered by the U.S. Environmental Protection Agency), first passed in 1974 and expanded and strengthened in 1986, protects the quality of drinking water. In the summer of 1994 the U.S. Congress began debate on further amendments to the Safe Drinking Water Act.

In Canada, drinking water is a shared federal-provincial responsibility. In general, provincial governments are responsible for an adequate, safe supply, whereas the Federal Department of National Health and Welfare develops water quality guidelines through a joint federal-provincial mechanism. These guidelines, however, are not legally enforceable unless adopted by a provincial agency. Two Canadian provinces, Alberta and Quebec, have adopted the federal guidelines as regulations.

110. *"Who enforces the federal standards?"*

In the United States, in general, your state health department has responsibility for enforcing the federal standards, although under certain circumstances another governmental agency may have that duty. Your water supplier can tell you who is responsible in your state. The states must adopt drinking water quality standards that are at least as strict as those of the federal government. Each state then evaluates its own water supplies and ranks them as **in compliance** or **out of compliance**. Of course, those out of compliance must be improved. A few states post signs at the city limits stating if the drinking water there is "in compliance."

In Canada, the appropriate provincial health and environmental agency has responsibility for the safety of drinking water and the application of the appropriate drinking water quality guidelines.

111. *"Is water that meets federal drinking water standards absolutely safe?"*

Safety is relative, not absolute. For example, an aspirin or two may help a headache, but if you took a whole bottle at once, you'd probably die. So, is aspirin safe? When setting drinking water standards, federal regulatory agencies use the concept of **reasonable risk**, not risk free. Risk-free water would cost too much. So the answer to the question is, no, drinking water isn't *absolutely* safe. But the likelihood of getting sick from drinking water that meets the federal standards is very small, typically one chance in a million.

One difficulty the U.S. Environmental Protection Agency has when trying to determine reasonable risk relates to the problem called **susceptible population**. Not all people who drink water are the same from a health point of view—that is, some people are more susceptible to getting sick than others. For example, only babies three months old or less are affected by nitrates in drinking water, so for that contaminant they are the susceptible population: they are susceptible to getting sick from too much nitrate in their drinking water. The standard for nitrate, therefore, was chosen to protect these infants. With other contaminants, identifying the susceptible population is not as easy. Are they the elderly, those undergoing cancer treatment, those in nursing homes, all babies, those who are HIV positive, or others? For each standard, the federal regulatory agencies must balance the risk to all these groups against the cost of treatment, and arrive at a standard that will protect as many people as possible and that can be afforded.

(See Question 20 for related information.)

112. *"How do federal regulatory agencies choose the standard for a chemical in drinking water?"*

Because rats and mice digest their food in the same way humans do, they are affected by toxic chemicals in the same way humans are. Therefore, scientists at the National Toxicology Program of the federal government feed these animals a chemical in question for a two-year period to determine its effect. From this information and using a safety factor, a drinking water standard based on "reasonable risk" is determined. For most potentially cancer-causing chemicals, reasonable risk is defined as follows: If one million people drank water for a period of seventy years with the amount of chemical in it equal to the standard, no more than one person would probably get cancer from the drinking water—a very small risk.

113. *"Most federal standards are written like this: 'Selenium— 0.05 mg/L.' What does 'mg/L' mean?"*

The abbreviation **mg/L** stands for milligrams per liter. In metric units, this is the weight of a chemical (selenium in the example) dissolved in a volume of water. One liter is about equal to one quart, and one ounce is equal to about 28,500 milligrams, so one milligram is a very small amount. About twenty-five grains of sugar weigh one milligram.

Because one liter of water weighs one million milligrams, one milligram per liter (mg/L) is sometimes written one part (weight of chemical) per million parts (weight of water), or one ppm (part per million). One part per million is hard to imagine. Here are some examples: 11.6 days contain one million seconds, so one second out of 11.6 days is one part per million (one second in a million seconds), or twenty-five grains of sugar in a quart of water is about one part per million, or one drop in a fifty-five-gallon drum is about one part per million. So you can see that the weight of selenium allowed by the federal government in a quart of water is very, very small. The limits set for some other chemicals in drinking water are even smaller. For example, the standard for cleaning fluid, a dangerous chemical, is only 0.002 mg/L (twenty-five times less than selenium). Chemicals with such severe limits are considered a serious health hazard.

If you would like a list of the federal regulations, look in Appendix A for the location of the U.S. Environmental Protection Agency office nearest you or for the Safe Drinking Water hotline telephone number.

114. *"Federal, state, provincial, and local governments will spend a lot of money over the next few years to satisfy the requirements of federal laws about drinking water quality. Will any lives be saved?"*

Much of the money will be spent to prevent germs from reaching consumers. Because germs in drinking water have caused deaths, improving microbial water quality could save some lives. Money also will be spent to remove cancer-causing chemicals from drinking water. The U.S. Environmental Protection Agency has estimated that 178 fewer cases of cancer will occur each year after water suppliers have satisfied the requirements of the federal laws. This is only an estimate because the specific cause of anyone's cancer is unknown.

Canadian authorities have not made similar predictions about the expected decline in cancer cases in their country.

(See Question 5 for related information.)

TESTING

115. *"How is my water tested, and who tests it?"*

Federal regulations state that all water suppliers must test the treated water for microbes and chemicals (a list of about ninety in the United States) a specified number of times each year. The tests for microbes are done most often; the frequency varies depending on the population served by a water supplier. Federal regulations in the United States also state that these tests must be conducted in federally certified laboratories using federally approved methods, some of which are quite complex. Canada does not require that tests be carried out in federally certified laboratories. Private wells are frequently tested in connection with the sale of a home.

116. *"Can I test my water at home?"*

Not in a meaningful way. Simple kits are available to test for some chemicals like chlorine, calcium, and lead, but a thorough analysis is not possible with these kits. In some cities, such as New York, water suppliers have begun offering free tests for lead in water.

The U.S. Environmental Protection Agency Safe Drinking Water hotline (see Appendix A) will send you a list of "State Certification Officers for Drinking Water Laboratories." This list gives the name of a person in each state who can give you information about testing laboratories in that state. The National Lead Information Center hotline (see Appendix A) is a good source of information on lead testing.

117. *"I have a private well. Who will test my water?"*

You can telephone your state, provincial, or local health department. Officials will help arrange to have your water tested, or they will explain how to take a sample for microbes and where you can take the sample for testing.

Larger cities have commercial laboratories that will

test drinking water for chemicals, but the tests are more expensive and often difficult to understand. The cost will depend on the type of tests you have done. A test for microbes (coliforms) will probably be less than ten dollars, but testing for chemicals can run into hundreds of dollars.

At the very minimum, you should have the water tested for lead, as well as coliforms, nitrate (particularly if you have or expect young children), radon, and arsenic.

(See Questions 13, 20, and 23 for related information.)

9.

Fantastic Facts

And more and more, the habit of keeping the coal in the bathtub is disappearing.

—H. Zinsser, Rats, Lice, and History

118. "How much water does one person use each day?"

Total water use varies depending on lawn watering, if any, and whether a home has a washing machine and dishwasher. The U.S. average is nearly 50 gallons used each day by each person. Of this, the amount used for cooking and drinking varies among individuals, from about 13 ounces to about 2 quarts. The average use is about 2½ pints—about half for plain water consumed as a beverage and the rest consumed in other beverages (e.g., juice, coffee, and so forth) and used for cooking.

Because of other uses in a community, the water supplier pumps much more water than is just used in households. A recent study of 1,100 water suppliers around the United States showed that to supply all the water needed for all uses, the average amount of water pumped was 180 gallons each day for each person.

In Canada, average total home water use is about 50 imperial gallons (60 U.S. gallons) for each person each day. The use for drinking only has been estimated at about 1.5 liters (1.6 quarts) each day.

(See Question 67 for related information.)

119. *"How much drinking water is produced in the entire United States each day, and how does that compare with the water used for irrigation of crops?"*

About 36.5 billion gallons of tap water is produced each day in the United States, 60 percent from surface water and 40 percent from groundwater. This is over 150 million tons of product each day. Daily irrigation use is much larger, but the volume depends on the location and the time of year. It takes about fifty glasses of water just to grow enough oranges to produce one glass of orange juice, for example. One estimate puts the total amount used for irrigation at 141 billion gallons a day, 66 percent from surface water and 34 percent from groundwater. Of course, irrigation water is not treated as tap water is.

(See Question 78 for related information.)

120. *"Does drinking water contain calories, fat, sugar, caffeine, or cholesterol?"*

No.

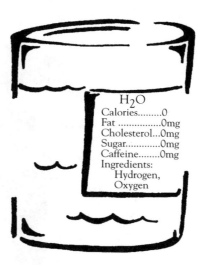

H_2O
Calories.........0
Fat 0mg
Cholesterol...0mg
Sugar.............0mg
Caffeine........0mg
Ingredients:
  Hydrogen,
  Oxygen

121. *"How heavy is water?"*

One U.S. gallon of water weighs about 8⅓ pounds. The imperial gallon used in Canada weighs 10 pounds. If you use 100 gallons of water in your home each day (a reasonable amount for two people), you are using more than 830 pounds of manufactured product each day, about 150 tons each year. A Canadian household of two would use about 180 tons of water each year, as on average they would use about the same number of gallons each day as the U.S. couple.

Water is so heavy that on a tonnage production basis the water supply industry is by far the largest in the United States and Canada. In the United States, it produces in sixteen hours as great a tonnage as the output of the oil industry in a year, in a single day as much tonnage as the steel industry does in an entire year, and in a week a tonnage equal to the yearly output of all of the bituminous coal producers—truly a monumental daily quantity of product.

122. *"I have a quarter-acre lot (180 feet by 60 feet). If it rains one inch, how much water falls on my lot?"*

About 7,000 U.S. gallons, or nearly 30 tons of water. If you had a half-acre lot, it would be twice as much, and so forth.

In Canada, 5,800 imperial gallons would fall during a one-inch rain, and the weight would still be measured as 30 tons.

123. *"What makes ice cubes cloudy?"* Commercially made ice is stirred as it is being frozen; household ice is not. Without mixing, many more ice crystals form, and air is trapped in the ice. Light rays are distorted by these crystals and air, and this distortion gives home-frozen ice a cloudy appearance.

124. *"Why do ice cubes bulge from the top of the ice-cube tray?"* Unlike most things, water gets bigger (expands) when it freezes. Because the ice-cube tray has a bottom and four sides that don't move, ice bulges out of the open top when the water gets bigger as it freezes.

Because frozen water (ice) is expanded, it is lighter than water. Therefore, in the winter, ice floats on the surface while the water underneath stays liquid, providing organisms, including fish, with a place to survive during the cold weather.

125. *"Which freezes faster, hot water or cold water?"* This is a trick question. Hot water placed in a freezer will freeze faster than cold water, but it's not really a fair race.

The hot water will freeze faster for two reasons. First, while the hot water is cooling down, some of it evaporates, so the amount of water to be frozen is less. Second, the warm container will melt any ice on the freezer coils under the container, thus making for better contact and more efficient freezing. Unfair, eh? Of course, you shouldn't use hot water for making ice cubes because of the contaminants that may be in it (see Question 45).

This "Fantastic Fact" was "discovered" many years ago when someone put two *wooden* buckets of water—

one filled with hot water, one with cold—outside on a very cold day. Because it took such a long time for the water to freeze, there was plenty of time for the hot water to evaporate while it was cooling. In your own freezer, if you use metal containers, the water may freeze so fast that you are not able to detect the effect. Open styrofoam containers should work better.

126. *"When I put ice cubes that I've made in my freezer in a glass of water, white stuff appears in the glass as they melt. What is the white stuff, and where does it come from?"*

Ice cubes freeze from the outside, so the center of the cube is the last to freeze. Ice is pure water, only H_2O, so as the ice cube freezes, all of the dissolved minerals, like the hardness minerals (see Question 54), are pushed to the center. Near the end of the freezing, there isn't much water left in the center of the cube, so these minerals become very concentrated, and they form the "white stuff"—the technical name is precipitate (pre·SIP·uh·tate). The hardness minerals that cause the "white stuff" are not toxic.

Some commercial ice cubes are "cored" after they freeze to remove this material. Having posts in your ice cube tray doesn't help, however, as the precipitate must actually be removed by coring.

127. *"What water does the president of the United States drink when in Washington, D.C., and when traveling abroad? What about the prime minister of Canada?"*

Wherever he is, the president drinks commercial bottled water, not because of concern about the quality of tap water in the United States, but to avoid any temporary mild discomfort that may occur from variations in the quality of perfectly safe drinking water from place to place. Thus, to ensure a constant drinking water quality both here and abroad, bottled water is supplied to the president.

The Canadian prime minister drinks tap water at home and bottled water when traveling outside Canada.

(See Question 36 for related information.)

128. *"Why are fire hydrants sometimes called fire plugs?"* Long ago, drinking water was distributed through towns in wooden pipes. When water was needed to fight a fire, a hole was drilled in the wooden pipe. When the fire was over, a wooden plug was used to close the hole. These **fire plugs** were then marked for possible future use.

Appendix A

Where Can I Get More Information?

READING MATERIAL

The following publications are available from the U.S. Environmental Protection Agency in Washington, DC, phone number (800) 426-4791:

Office of Groundwater and Drinking Water Publications, EPA/810/B-94/001, Jan., 1994 (complete list of titles to date)

SELECTED TITLES FROM EPA/810/8-94/001:

- *Lead and Your Drinking Water*, EPA/810-F-93-001, June, 1993
- *Home Water Treatment Units—Filtering Fact from Fiction*, EPA 570/9-90-HHH, September, 1990
- *Drinking Water from Household Wells*, EPA 570/9-90-013, September, 1990
- *Bottled Water: Helpful Facts and Information*, EPA 570/9-90-GGG, September, 1990
- *Pesticides in Drinking Water Wells*, EPA 20T-1004, revised September, 1990
- *Is Your Drinking Water Safe?* EPA 570/9-91- 005, September, 1991
- *The Safe Drinking Water Act*, September, 1990
- *Lead in School Drinking Water*, EPA 570/9-89- 001, January, 1989
- *Lead in School Drinking Water—A Manual for Schools and Day Care Centers*, USEPA, Office of Water, April, 1989
- *EPA Cross-connection Manual*, EPA 570/9-89- 007, September, 1989

The booklet *Drinking Water: Inadequate Regulation of Home Treatment Units Leaves Consumers at Risk* (December, 1991-RECD-92-34) is available from:

> U.S. General Accounting Office
> P.O. Box 6015
> Gaithersburg, MD 20884
> (202) 512-6000

Two consumers' booklets are available from the U.S. Federal Trade Commission, Bureau of Consumer Protection, Office of Consumer/Business Education, Washington, DC 20580, phone (202) 326-3650:
° *Buying a Home Water Treatment Unit,* August, 1989
° *Water Testing Scams,* August, 1990

The American Ground Water Trust has published a booklet (1991), *When You Need a Water Well*:

> 6375 Riverside Drive
> Dublin, OH 43017
> (800) 332-2104

OTHER SOURCES

In the United States, write to:
> Office of Groundwater and Drinking Water
> U.S. Environmental Protection Agency (4601)
> 401 M Street, S.W.
> Washington, DC 20460

or call its toll-free safe drinking water hotline
> (800) 426-4791
> (9:00 A.M. to 5:30 P.M. Eastern Time, Monday through Friday)

or contact
> Technical Support Division
> Office of Groundwater and Drinking Water
> U.S. Environmental Protection Agency
> 26 W. Martin Luther King Drive
> Cincinnati, OH 45268
> (513) 569-7904.

In Canada, write to:
> Health and Welfare Canada
> Tunney's Pasture
> Ottawa, Canada K1A 0L2.

Calling your local water supplier can often provide answers to many of your questions specific to your own system.

In the United States, you can also contact your regional U.S. Environmental Protection Agency office:

• Region 1— Connecticut, Maine, Massachusetts, New Hampshire, Rhode Island, Vermont
> Water Supply Section
> US EPA Region I
> JFK Federal Bldg.-WSS
> Boston, MA 02203
> (617) 565-3610

• Region 2—New Jersey, New York, Puerto Rico, U.S. Virgin Islands
> Public Water Supply Section
> USEPA Region II
> 26 Federal Plaza, Room 853
> New York, NY 10278
> (212) 264-1800

• Region 3—Delaware, District of Columbia, Maryland, Pennsylvania, Virginia, West Virginia
> Drinking Water Section
> USEPA Region III
> 841 Chestnut Street, Room 3WM40
> Philadelphia, PA 19107
> (215) 597-8227

• Region 4 —Alabama, Florida, Georgia, Kentucky, Mississippi, North Carolina, South Carolina, Tennessee
> Drinking Water Section
> USEPA Region IV
> 345 Courtland Street, N.E.
> Atlanta, GA 30365
> (404) 347-2913

•Region 5—Illinois, Indiana, Michigan, Minnesota, Ohio, Wisconsin

> Drinking Water Section
> US EPA Region V
> 77 W. Jackson Boulevard
> Chicago, IL 60604-3590
> (312) 886-6206

• Region 6 —Arkansas, Louisiana, New Mexico, Oklahoma, Texas

> PWS Section
> US EPA Region VI
> 1445 Ross Avenue
> Dallas, TX 75202-2733
> (214) 665-7155

• Region 7—Iowa, Kansas, Missouri, Nebraska

> Drinking Water Section
> US EPA Region VII WATR / DRNK
> 726 Minnesota Avenue
> Kansas City, KS 66101
> (913) 551-7032

• Region 8 — Colorado, Montana, North Dakota, South Dakota, Utah, Wyoming

> PWSP Section
> US EPA Region VIII 8WM-DW
> 999 18th Street, Suite 500
> Denver, CO 80202-2466
> (303) 293-1413

• Region 9—Arizona, California, Hawaii, Nevada, American Samoa, Guam, Trust Territories of the Pacific

> Drinking Water Section (W-6-1)
> US EPA Region IX
> 75 Hawthorne Street
> San Francisco, CA 94105
> (415) 744-1851

- Region 10 —Alaska, Idaho, Oregon, Washington
      Drinking Water Section
      US EPA Region X (WD-132)
      1200 Sixth Avenue
      Seattle, WA 98101
      (206) 553-1224

Another good source of information is:
      American Water Works Association
      6666 W. Quincy Avenue
      Denver, CO 80235-3098
      (303) 794-7711

Educators, ask for the Public Affairs Department. You may also call:
      (800) 366-0107— Small Systems hotline
      (800) 559-9855— WaterWiser: The Water Efficiency Clearinghouse
      (800) 926-7337— for the AWWA book on conservation (Item No. 10063), other publications, or a free Publications Catalog.

Below are listed several other national hotlines and clearinghouses on environmental issues:
- Asbestos Ombudsman Office (USEPA) (800) 368-5888
- Hazardous Waste Ombudsman (800) 262-7937
- Indoor Air Quality Information Center (800) 438-4318
- National Lead Information Center (800) 424-5323
- National Pesticides Telecommunications Network hotline (800) 858-7378
- National Radon hotline (800) 767-7236
- National Response Center hotline (to report spills of oil and other hazardous materials) (800) 424-8802
- National Small Flows Clearinghouse (800) 624-8301
- Office of Environmental Justice hotline (800) 962-6215
- Pollution Prevention Information Clearinghouse (202) 260-1023
- Storm-water hotline (703) 821-4823
- USEPA Acid Rain hotline (202) 233-9620
- USEPA Wetlands Protection hotline (800) 832-7828

Appendix B

Complete Listing
of Questions by Chapter

CHAPTER 1. HEALTH

General

1. Is my water safe to drink?
2. Can I tell if my drinking water is okay by just looking at it, tasting it, or smelling it?
3. How do I find out if my water is safe to drink?
4. I've received a notice from my water utility telling me that something is wrong. What's that all about? What is a "boil water order?"
5. Does anyone actually get sick from drinking water?
6. I have read about animals dying after drinking reservoir water. If this can happen, how can I be sure my drinking water is safe?
7. They let people swim and go boating in our reservoir. Should I worry about this?
8. Is tap water suitable for use in a home kidney dialysis machine?
9. Is it true that people who take antacids regularly are more likely to get sick from drinking water?
10. When I'm working in the yard, I'm tempted to take a drink from my garden hose. Is this safe?

Germs

11. Is my drinking water completely free of microbes?
12. How are germs that can make me sick kept out of my drinking water?
13. I'm told that I shouldn't drink my well water or that I need to boil it because my water has coliforms in it, but I'm also told that coliforms are harmless. Then I read that food poisoning can occur because of coliforms in meat. What are coliforms, and what's going on?

14. If I want to kill all the germs in my drinking water, what should I do?
15. Could my drinking water transmit the AIDS virus?

Chemicals

General

16. Are all chemicals in my drinking water bad for me?
17. Are chemicals that are found in drinking water naturally (rather than because of pollution) nontoxic?
18. I read that organic chemicals are bad for my health. What are they, why are they dangerous, and why doesn't my water utility just remove them?
19. I'm told that our drinking water contains chemicals like cleaning fluid and benzene. What can I do about this while the water company is improving treatment?
20. I've heard that nitrates are bad for infants, and pesticides are bad for everyone. How do nitrates and pesticides get into my drinking water?
21. There is a blue-green stain where my water drips into my sink. What causes this?
22. Do hazardous wastes contaminate drinking water?

Lead

23. How does lead get into my drinking water?
24. How can I get lead out of my drinking water?
25. How can I find out if my water is supplied through lead pipes?
26. Is it safe to drink water from a drinking fountain?

Fluoride

27. Is the fluoride in my drinking water safe?

Chlorine

28. Is water with chlorine in it safe to drink?
29. What is the link between chlorine and cancer?

Aluminum

30. I hear aluminum is used to treat drinking water. Is this a problem?

Does it cause Alzheimer's disease?

31. Is it safe to cook with aluminum pans?

Radon

32. What is radon, and is it harmful in drinking water?

33. I'm worried that my drinking water has radon in it and that the radon will get into the air in my home. How can I test the air in my home for radon?

34. Will a water softener take radon and radium out of my water?

Travel

35. I travel overseas. In which countries is the water safe to drink?

36. When I travel to a different place in this country, sometimes I have an upset stomach for a couple of days. Is this because something is wrong with the water?

37. Is it okay for hikers, campers, and backpackers to drink water from remote streams?

38. What can hikers, campers, and backpackers do to treat stream water to make it safe to drink?

CHAPTER 2. AESTHETICS

Taste and Odor

39. Why does my drinking water taste or smell "funny," and will this smelly water make me sick?

40. What can I do if my drinking water tastes "funny?"

Appearance

41. Drinking water often looks cloudy when first taken from a faucet, and then it clears up. Why is that?

42. My drinking water is reddish or brown. What causes this?

43. My drinking water is dark in color, nearly black. What causes this?

CHAPTER 3. HOME FACTS

General

44. How long can I store drinking water?
45. Is it okay to use hot water from the tap for cooking?
46. What causes the banging or popping noise that some water heaters, radiators, and pipes make?
47. Why do hot water heaters fail?
48. How should I fill my fish aquarium?
49. Where does the water go when it goes down the drain?
50. What can I safely pour down the sink or into the toilet?

Treatment

51. Should I install home water treatment equipment?
52. I bought a water filter for my house, and after six months when I went to change it, the filter was covered with gunk. Is my drinking water really okay with all that stuff in it?
53. When a piece of home water treatment equipment bears a label that says, "Registered by the U.S. Environmental Protection Agency," does this mean that the EPA has tested the equipment and that it is effective?

Hard and Soft Water

54. What is "hard" water?
55. Should I install a water softener in my home?
56. What is that white stuff in my coffeepot and on my shower head and glass shower door? How can I get rid of it?
57. Why does my dishwater leave spots on my glasses?
58. What causes the whitish layer on the soil of my potted plants?

Bottled Water

59. Should I buy bottled water?
60. What do the various labels on bottled water mean?
61. Is distilled water the "perfect" drinking water?
62. Should I buy drinking water from a vending machine?

Cost

63. What is the cost of the water I use in my home?

64. How does a water company know how much water I use in my home?

65. How does the water company know that my water meter is correct?

66. We had a conservation drive in our area, and everyone cooperated. Then our water rates went up. Why?

CHAPTER 4. CONSERVATION

67. What activity in my home uses the most water?

68. Some people say I should put a brick in my toilet tank to save water. How does that save water, and is this a good idea?

69. I heard that it's a good idea to control the flow of water from my showerhead. How do I measure how fast my shower is using water?

70. Why are there aerators on home water faucets?

71. I leave the water running while I'm brushing my teeth. Does that waste much water?

72. Many water quality problems in the home—lead, red water, sand in the system, and so forth—are cured by flushing the system. But isn't that a waste of water?

73. My water faucet drips a little; should I bother to fix it?

74. How should I water my lawn to avoid wasting water?

75. Why do we still have a water shortage when it's been raining at my house?

76. During times of water shortages, shouldn't decorative fountains be turned off?

77. During times of water shortage, does not serving water to restaurant customers really help?

CHAPTER 5. SOURCES

General

78. Where does my drinking water come from?

79. Are we running out of water?

80. How does nature recycle water?

81. When I see pictures of the earth from outer space, it looks like it's mostly covered with water. Is that right, and how much of this water is drinkable?

82. Many areas near the ocean do not have large supplies of fresh water. Why can't ocean water be treated to make drinking water?

83. Can wastewater be treated to make it into drinking water?

Quality

84. Which is more polluted, groundwater or surface water?

85. In towns and cities, what is the major cause of pollution of drinking water sources?

86. Why isn't urban runoff usually treated before being discharged into drinking water sources?

87. Does acid rain affect water supplies?

88. I read about the problem of oil spills. Do they pollute drinking water sources?

89. How can I help prevent pollution of drinking water sources?

90. Why does my water sometimes have sand in it?

CHAPTER 6. SUPPLIERS

91. How many drinking water suppliers are there in the United States and Canada?

92. Are all drinking water utilities owned by cities and towns?

93. How is my drinking water treated?

94. Is it true that some major cities do not filter their drinking water?

95. I've read all about the problems with my drinking water. Why isn't my water supplier doing something about it?

CHAPTER 7. DISTRIBUTION

CHAPTER 8. REGULATIONS AND TESTING

Federal Regulations

112. How do federal regulatory agencies choose the standard for a chemical in drinking water?

113. Most federal standards are written like this: "Selenium—0.05 mg/L." What does "mg/L" mean?

114. Federal, state, provincial, and local governments will spend a lot of money over the next few years to satisfy the requirements of federal laws about drinking water quality. Will any lives be saved?

Testing

115. How is my water tested, and who tests it?

116. Can I test my water at home?

117. I have a private well. Who will test my water?

CHAPTER 9. FANTASTIC FACTS

118. How much water does one person use each day?

119. How much drinking water is produced in the entire United States each day, and how does that compare with the water used for irrigation of crops?

120. Does drinking water contain calories, fat, sugar, caffeine, or cholesterol?

121. How heavy is water?

122. I have a quarter-acre lot (180 feet by 60 feet). If it rains one inch, how much water falls on my lot?

123. What makes ice cubes cloudy?

124. Why do ice cubes bulge from the top of the ice-cube tray?

125. Which freezes faster, hot water or cold water?

126. When I put ice cubes that I've made in my freezer in a glass of water, white stuff appears in the glass as they melt. What is the white stuff, and where does it come from?

127. What water does the president of the United States drink when in Washington, D.C., and when traveling abroad? What about the prime minister of Canada?

128. Why are fire hydrants sometimes called fire plugs?

Index